IUL

THE SECRET TO TAX-FREE RETIREMENT AND GENERATIONAL WEALTH.

Wilken Dorcilien

Scan the code to book a call for IUL consultations:

Disclaimer

This book is for informational and educational purposes only and does not constitute financial, legal, or tax advice. The concepts and strategies discussed, including Indexed Universal Life (IUL) policies, may not be suitable for everyone. Readers should consult with a licensed financial professional, tax advisor, or legal expert before making any financial decisions. The author and publisher are not responsible for any financial outcomes resulting from the application of the information in this book. All investments carry risks, and past performance is not a guarantee of future results.

Why Index Universal Life?

Let's say you have $100,000. What would you do with it?

Some people say they would start a business. Others might invest in real estate or the stock market. All of these are great ideas, and they have the potential to generate wealth. But let's consider what happens if life takes an unexpected turn.

What if the business fails? What if the real estate market crashes? What if the stock market takes a major dip and wipes out a significant portion of your investment? In that case, what's left? The answer is simple—whatever is left after the loss, and for many, that could mean nothing.

Now, let's take it a step further. Imagine that after investing the $100,000, the investor—let's call him Mr. X—suffers a stroke or, even worse, passes away unexpectedly. His family is left to liquidate the business, real estate, or stocks at a lower price just to get some money to survive. Instead of leaving behind security, Mr. X's financial decisions may now create stress and hardship for his loved ones.

I love all of these investments—business, real estate, and stocks—but I would approach them differently. Instead of risking my money from the start, I would first secure it. Here's what I would do:

I would take that $100,000 and place it into an **Indexed Universal Life (IUL) policy**. Then, I would borrow against the policy's cash value to fund my investments.

Why is this a smarter move?

- **If my investment succeeds, I win twice**—I benefit from the returns on my investment while my original $100,000 remains safe inside the IUL, growing with **compounding interest**.
- **If my investment fails, I don't actually lose**—because my $100,000 is still inside the IUL, protected and growing tax-free. I may not be able to take another loan right away, but as my policy gains interest over time, I can borrow again.
- **If something happens to me, my family is protected**—because an IUL provides a **death benefit**, leaving my loved ones with **far more than the original $100,000**.

This is why I say that an **IUL is like a financial fortress**—a place where you can **secure your money before you risk it in any other market**.

As you continue reading this book, you will gain a deeper understanding of why the **IUL strategy is a powerful tool for both wealth-building and financial security**.

A Clash of Perspectives – The Conversation That Tested Me

It was a typical Friday, or so I thought. February 21, 2025—just another day of helping a client secure their financial future with an Indexed Universal Life (IUL) policy. But that day took an unexpected turn when my client introduced me to their financial advisor. The client wanted me to meet with him for some clarifications, and I was more than happy to do so.

At first, the conversation felt routine, but it quickly turned into something else—an interrogation.

We exchanged introductions, and before long, the advisor leaned in and asked, **"Do you have a license to sell this product?"**

"Yes, sir," I replied confidently. Then he said, **for full disclosure, I have all the securities licenses. I have been in this business for so many years. I know about everything that has to do with investment.**

Then came the follow-up: **"Do you have a securities license?"**

"No, sir."

His expression tightened. **"Do you know that you need a securities license to sell an IUL?"**

That was the moment I realized this wasn't a friendly exchange—it was a challenge.

“No, you don't need a securities license to sell an IUL,” I said firmly. **“And if that were the case, the government would regulate it.”**

I could sense something in his tone, something that didn't sit right. Was he questioning my integrity? Did he think I was operating outside the law? The conversation took on an almost interrogative nature, making me wonder if I was on trial instead of having a professional discussion.

Then he hit me with another question. **“Why did you sell the client a $150,000 policy when they could get a $500,000 policy for nearly the same cost? Why did you sell the client a $150K policy that could cost $120 for $500?”**

I took a deep breath and responded, **“That's the beauty of a well-designed IUL. It allows the client to contribute more money into the policy that goes toward the cash value. If I had given the client a $500K policy for that price, he wouldn't have had enough money going toward his retirement planning. The focus here isn't just the death benefit—it's wealth accumulation and financial security during retirement.”**

I could tell he wasn't satisfied with my answer. He leaned in again and asked another question.

"Why didn't you just put the client in a mutual fund and give them a term policy for $100?"

At this point, my voice started to change. "Because mutual funds are directly connected to the market. When the market goes up, it follows. But when the market crashes, you lose money. Unlike mutual funds, an IUL takes advantage of the market's growth, and when the market goes down, it locks the account so that the client doesn't lose money."

But he still wasn't done.

"Why did you have to sell two policies?"

I furrowed my brows. "What do you mean?"

"You sold the client one policy and the spouse a separate one. Why didn't you just add a spouse rider? They would have paid less."

At this point, I was stunned. "Sir, did you know that a spouse rider does not keep the policy if the primary insured passes away?"

Without hesitation, he responded, "Yes, the rider will keep the policy even if the insured passes away."

Now I was the one in shock. "No, it doesn't! If the primary insured dies, the rider does not convert into a standalone policy. The coverage for the spouse is gone."

I took a deep breath before continuing, "The other reason we did two policies is that each person needs their own retirement plan. The more money they are able to contribute into their policy, the better for their retirement."

At that point, my voice had risen. I wasn't just explaining anymore—I was defending my expertise.

And then came another question.

"What is the rate of return the client will receive?"

I calmly replied, "It depends on the performance of the indexes we select."

"Who selects the index?" he shot back.

"I do."

"Why doesn't the client select the indexes?"

At that moment, I looked at him and said, "You are really testing me. I know you know the answer, and I'm not answering that."

I was about to take off my jacket and do some pushups to get ready for a fight, but then I realized—we were in a virtual meeting room.

The tension was thick. I was beginning to wonder what this conversation was really about. Was he asking these questions because he genuinely didn't know, or was he testing me? And if he was testing me, why?

But then, in the last five minutes, something changed. The conversation cooled down. The intensity faded, and we started having a more level-headed discussion. By the end, we even agreed to meet again.

Maybe, just maybe, this could be the start of a great professional relationship.

Lessons Learned:

- **Always be patient.** Not everyone understands how an IUL works, and it's my job to educate—not argue.
- **Not even financial professionals know everything.** Even licensed advisors can have gaps in their understanding of certain financial products.
- **Some conversations feel like battles, but they can turn into bridges.** The last five minutes of our talk

> cooled down, and we agreed to meet again. This might just be the beginning of a great relationship.

If I meet with him again before finishing this book, I'll be sure to update you on how it all ended.

Looking back, I know I could have handled it differently. But in that moment, it felt less like a conversation and more like a courtroom cross-examination.

To **Mr. R. W., if you're reading this**, I want to say—I am sorry, I could have responded better. I let frustration creep in where patience should have remained. But I still don't understand why this conversation took that turn.

I share this with you, dear reader, because this conversation will clarify a lot of questions you may have about IULs. I still don't know what was on the back of the mind of the financial advisor, but it worked for good.

AKNOWLEDGMENT

First, I thank God for providing the wisdom, strength, and resources to create and build. Without His guidance, none of this would be possible.

A huge thank you to Team Legacy and Team Aqua for your support and belief in this mission. Your dedication fuels my drive.

Special thanks to Rose Apollon from Liberation of Self for your mentorship and partnership—your guidance has been invaluable.

To my beautiful wife, Anna, thank you for your unwavering support. To my amazing kids—Benley, Audrey, and Gabriel—you are my greatest motivation.

Much gratitude to David Shands for your mentorship and leadership—teaching me that consistency is the ultimate cheat code for success.

To everyone who has supported this vision—thank you. This book is about knowledge, discipline, and proving that It's Possible

Contents

PREFACE

The way people think about money plays a crucial role in determining their financial destiny. Mindset is everything when it comes to wealth-building, yet most people operate within limiting beliefs that keep them stuck in a financial cycle they can't escape. People with a poor mindset believe that money exists simply to pay bills. Their goal each month is just to make ends meet, and as long as the rent is paid, the lights are on, and there's food on the table, they feel they are financially stable. They don't think beyond their immediate needs, and because of this limited vision, they never seek ways to grow their income or build wealth. These individuals often live paycheck to paycheck, never planning for the future, and accepting financial struggle as a normal part of life. They are trapped in survival mode, believing that as long as they can cover their expenses, they are doing "just fine," without realizing that this mindset prevents them from ever experiencing true financial security or freedom.

The middle-class mindset, while slightly more financially comfortable, is also deeply flawed. People with this mentality believe that money is meant to buy things. They associate wealth with possessions—expensive cars, designer clothes, the latest technology, and lavish vacations. They may look rich on the outside, but in reality, they are often drowning in debt. They finance their lifestyle with credit cards and loans, constantly chasing the illusion of wealth rather than building real financial security. Many middle-class individuals earn a good salary, yet they still struggle financially because they spend everything they make (and often more). Their focus is on consuming rather than investing, and because of this, they remain in the same financial position year after year. They work hard to earn more money, only to immediately spend it on depreciating assets. The middle-class mindset values comfort over financial freedom, making decisions based on short-term gratification rather than long-term financial growth.

On the other hand, the wealthy mindset views money in an entirely different way. Wealthy individuals understand that money's primary purpose is not just to pay bills or buy things but to make more money. They see money as a tool—something that, when used wisely, can multiply and create generational wealth. The wealthy believe that their money should work for them, not the other way around. Instead of spending every dollar they earn, they focus on investing in assets that appreciate over time, such as businesses, stocks, real estate, and financial vehicles like

Indexed Universal Life (IUL) policies. They understand the power of compounding interest and passive income, allowing their money to generate returns and build wealth effortlessly. While poor and middle-class individuals work for money, the wealthy make sure their money works for them.

One of the key differences in mindset is that the wealthy see money as a seed, not just as a means to survive or a way to display success. They know that if they plant their money wisely—investing in income-producing assets—it will grow and multiply. They also understand the importance of delayed gratification, resisting the urge to spend money impulsively in favor of making strategic financial decisions that will benefit them in the long run. This is why the rich continue to get richer: they prioritize wealth-building strategies over lifestyle inflation. Rather than keeping their money sitting in a low-interest savings account or spending it on liabilities, they direct their resources toward opportunities that will provide consistent returns.

Your mindset ultimately determines your relationship with money and your financial future. If you see money only as a means to cover bills, you will always be struggling financially. If you see it as a way to buy material things, you may look successful but will remain financially unstable. However, if you adopt the mindset of the wealthy—

believing that money should be used to create more money—you will put yourself on the path to financial independence. The way you think about money dictates the choices you make, and those choices will determine whether you remain financially stuck or break free from the cycle of struggle. The key is to shift your mindset, embrace financial education, and start seeing money as a tool for wealth creation rather than just survival or consumption

Introduction

THE TIME TO PLAN IS NOW

Who should be planning for retirement? The answer is simple: everyone.

Even before a person is born, there should be a financial plan in place for their future—including retirement. But let's be honest: **we don't know many people who do that.** Most of us were born into families that were just trying to survive, not thinking about financial independence decades down the line. However, that doesn't change the fact that from the moment you take your first breath, **time starts ticking—and it never moves backward.**

During childhood and teenage years, you don't have control over financial decisions. That responsibility falls on your parents. **But did they prepare you for financial success?** Did they teach you about investing, saving, and building wealth? For most people, the answer is no.

The reality is, many parents simply **didn't know what they didn't know.** They weren't given financial education, and as a result, they couldn't pass it down to the next generation. But if your parents didn't have the knowledge or the resources to set you up for success, **that excuse stops with you**. Now, it's your turn.

If you were born poor, that's not your fault. If you retire poor, that is your fault.

It doesn't matter how old you are today—whether you're in your 20s, 40s, or even 60s—**you need to be planning for your retirement.** And the good news? It's never too late to start.

This book will **equip you with the right mindset, tools, and strategies** to ensure that when your working years come to an end, you can retire stress-free. You'll learn about different retirement vehicles, why **an Index Universal Life (IUL) policy can be a powerful tool**, and how to build wealth that lasts for generations.

The most important thing to remember is this: **Retirement isn't an age. It's a financial position.** And starting today, you're taking control of your future.

Retirement in America is becoming an increasingly uncertain and frightening time for millions of people due to inadequate savings, rising living costs, and a lack of financial preparedness. Studies show that a significant percentage of Americans retire in poverty, struggle with financial insecurity, and face an uphill battle in maintaining their standard of living after they stop working. According to the U.S. Census Bureau, around 10.2% of adults aged 65 and older—approximately 5.9 million seniors—live below the poverty line, which, as of 2024, is set at an annual income of $14,040 for an individual. Many more retirees live just above this threshold, making them vulnerable to economic downturns, medical expenses, and rising inflation. Social Security, which was designed as a supplemental income rather than a primary retirement plan, has become the sole source of income for approximately 40% of retirees. However, the average monthly Social Security check in 2024 is only about $1,837, or roughly $22,044 per year—far from enough to cover basic living expenses in most parts of the country.

One of the main reasons so many Americans face financial struggles in retirement is that they simply do not have enough savings. A study by the Employee Benefit Research Institute (EBRI) found that nearly 40% of Americans aged 55 and older have less than $50,000 in retirement savings, and a shocking 25% have no retirement savings at all. Experts generally recommend that retirees should have savings that can replace at least 70% to 80% of their pre-retirement income, yet many fall drastically short of this target. The National Institute on Retirement Security (NIRS) reports that the median retirement savings balance for American households nearing retirement is just $10,000—a number far below what is needed to ensure financial security in later years.

The financial crisis among retirees is directly tied to the broader issue of Americans living paycheck to paycheck. A 2024 report from LendingClub found that 62% of U.S. adults—across all income levels—live paycheck to paycheck, meaning they have little to no emergency savings. This problem isn't just affecting low-income earners; even among those earning over $100,000 per year, nearly 45% report that they are struggling to make ends meet. Rising inflation, stagnant wages, and increased costs for housing, healthcare, and everyday essentials have made it difficult for workers to save for the future. With little to no savings to fall back on, many Americans enter retirement without a financial cushion, making them highly dependent on Social Security and at risk of falling into poverty.

Another growing concern is the rising cost of healthcare in retirement. According to Fidelity Investments, the average 65-year-old couple retiring today will need approximately $315,000 to cover healthcare expenses throughout retirement. For many retirees, these costs alone can deplete their savings rapidly. Long-term care, which is not fully covered by Medicare, can cost between $50,000 and $100,000 per year, depending on the level of care needed. Without sufficient savings or long-term care insurance, retirees often find themselves facing severe financial hardship due to medical expenses.

Furthermore, the traditional retirement age of 65 is becoming less realistic for many Americans. Because they cannot afford to stop working, an increasing number of people are delaying retirement or re-entering the workforce after retiring. A study by the Bureau of Labor Statistics (BLS) projects that by 2030, nearly one in four workers will be over the age of 65. This trend highlights the financial pressure that many older adults face as they struggle to make ends meet. The fear of outliving their savings is a major concern, with the average life expectancy in the U.S. now reaching around 77 years. Many retirees worry about depleting their funds, especially with the uncertainties of market volatility, inflation, and potential reductions in Social Security benefits.

Ultimately, these statistics paint a sobering picture of the state of retirement in America. Without proper financial planning, many retirees are forced to make difficult choices, such as cutting back on necessities, downsizing their homes, or even returning to work. The reality is that the current system is failing to provide a secure financial future for millions of Americans, making it more critical than ever for individuals to take proactive steps to secure their retirement. Whether through better saving habits, investing in tax-advantaged accounts like IUL policies, or seeking financial education, the need for long-term planning has never been greater.

Chapter

1

THE RETIREMENT CRISIS – WHY TRADITIONAL PLANS ARE FAILING

For decades, Americans have been told the same story about retirement: **Work hard, save in a 401(k) or IRA, and one day, you'll have enough to retire comfortably.** But that traditional model is crumbling, and millions of retirees are finding themselves in financial distress.

The Biggest Challenges Retirees Face Today

Retirement is no longer as simple as it once was. The world has changed, and failing to adapt can mean facing a financial disaster in your golden years. Here are some of the **biggest threats to retirement today:**

1. Market Volatility – Your Savings Are Not Guaranteed

Most traditional retirement accounts—401(k)s, IRAs, and even pensions—are heavily tied to the stock market. While the market has historically trended upward over time, it does not **move in a straight line**. Economic downturns, recessions, and crashes can **wipe out years of savings overnight**.

Example: In 2008, the stock market crashed by nearly 40%, and millions of Americans lost half their retirement savings. Many who planned to retire had to **keep working for another decade** just to recover.

If your financial future is completely dependent on the market, **you're taking a massive risk.**

2. Rising Taxes – The Silent Wealth Killer

When you save money in a **401(k) or traditional IRA**, you are **not avoiding taxes—you're just postponing them.**

Right now, tax rates may seem reasonable, but they are historically **low**. With the national debt increasing and government spending at an all-time high, **where do you think future tax rates are headed?**

Think about this: If you retire with $1 million in a 401(k) but tax rates increase to 40%, **you only get to keep**

$600,000. You didn't plan to lose 40% of your wealth, but Uncle Sam did.

If your retirement plan doesn't **protect you from future tax hikes**, you could end up with far less than you expected.

3. Inflation – The Silent Retirement Thief

Inflation erodes the value of money over time. What **$1,000** could buy you today won't be the same in 20 or 30 years.

Example: In 1990, the average cost of a new car was **$9,400**. Today, that same car would cost over **$40,000.**

If you don't have a retirement plan that accounts for inflation, you may **run out of money faster than you thought.**

4. Longevity – Outliving Your Savings

People are living longer than ever. While that sounds great, it creates a major problem: **Will your money last as long as you do?**

The facts:

- In 1950, the average life expectancy was **68 years.**
- Today, it's closer to **80 years**—and many people live well into their 90s.

If your retirement plan was built for 20 years of retirement but you live for 30 or 40 years after you stop working, **how will you cover the extra decades?**

The Solution: A Smarter Approach to Retirement

The truth is, **traditional retirement plans are broken.** Depending on the stock market, government tax policies, and unpredictable inflation is **not a strategy—it's a gamble.**

Why Social Security and 401(k)s Are Not Enough

For decades, Americans have relied on two major sources for retirement: **Social Security and 401(k)s.** But here's the truth—**neither is enough to retire comfortably anymore.** Let's break it down.

---

1. Social Security – A Failing Safety Net

Social Security was designed in 1935 as a safety net to help retirees, but it was never meant to be a full retirement plan. Back then, life expectancy was **around 60-65 years**, and people didn't live long after retiring. **Today, people are living 20-30 years in retirement, and Social Security is running out of money.**

The Facts:

- The Social Security Trust Fund is projected to **run out by 2034** if no changes are made.
- The average monthly Social Security check in 2023 was **$1,827**—barely enough to cover rent and groceries.
- Future benefits may be **reduced** if the system isn't fixed.

Many retirees **assumed** Social Security would cover their expenses, only to find themselves struggling. **If you rely on Social Security alone, you will likely fall short.**

---

2. 401(k)s – The Hidden Dangers No One Talks About

Most people have been told to **save in a 401(k) and let it grow over time.** But there are several **big problems** with this approach that many don't realize until it's too late.

Problem #1: The Market Controls Your Retirement

401(k)s are directly tied to the **stock market.** That means when the market crashes, **so does your retirement savings.**

Example: In 2008, the market crashed by almost **40%,** wiping out trillions in retirement accounts. Many people had to **delay retirement for years** just to recover.

If the market crashes right before you retire, **you may not have enough time to rebuild.**

Problem #2: You Don't Control Your Taxes

A 401(k) is a **tax-deferred account**, meaning you don't pay taxes now—but you do when you retire. The problem? **You have no idea what tax rates will be in the future.**

Consider this:

- If you retire with **$1 million in your 401(k)**, but tax rates are at 35%, you only get **$650,000**—the rest goes to the IRS.
- The government can **change tax rates anytime**, and retirees will be the ones paying the price.

Problem #3: Required Minimum Distributions (RMDs)

The government forces you to start **withdrawing from your 401(k) at age** 73, whether you need the money or not. And if you don't withdraw enough, **you get hit with a 25% penalty!**

In short: The government controls when and how you can use your money.

What's the Alternative? A Smarter Retirement Strategy

If Social Security and 401(k)s are **not enough**, what's the solution? **You need a retirement plan that is:**

- **Protected from market losses**
- **Tax-free in retirement**
- **Flexible, so you control your money**
- **Designed to last a lifetime**

This is why **high-income earners and the wealthy** use **Index Universal Life (IUL) insurance** as part of their retirement strategy

How Inflation, Taxes, and Healthcare Costs Eat Into Your Savings

Even if you have diligently saved for retirement, three major financial forces will erode your wealth over time: **inflation, taxes, and healthcare costs.** Let's break down how each of these can impact your financial future.

---

1. Inflation – The Silent Wealth Killer

Inflation is the gradual increase in the cost of goods and services over time. While 2-3% inflation may not seem like a big deal in one year, **over decades, it drastically reduces your purchasing power.**

The Facts:

- In 1990, a gallon of gas cost around **$1.16**. Today, it's **over $3.50** in many places.
- The average new car price in 2000 was **$21,850.** Today, it's **over $48,000.**
- A retiree living on **$50,000 a year today** will need **over $90,000 a year in 25 years** just to maintain the same lifestyle.

If your retirement savings don't **outpace inflation**, your money will lose value over time.

What does this mean for you?

- If your retirement plan assumes today's cost of living, **you will run out of money faster than expected.**
- You need **investments and financial products that grow and keep up with inflation.**

---

2. Taxes – The Hidden Cost of Your Retirement Savings

Many people assume they will pay **less in taxes** when they retire. But the truth is, tax rates could go **up**, not down. And if most of your money is in **a 401(k) or traditional** IRA, you still have to pay **income tax** on every dollar you withdraw.

The Reality About Taxes in Retirement:

- **Tax rates are historically low right now**—but what happens when the government raises taxes to cover national debt?
- If you retire with a **$1 million** 401(k), you don't really have $1 million—you still owe **taxes** on it!
- Withdraw too much, and you could get bumped into a **higher tax bracket**, paying more than you expected.

IRS Codes That Favor the Wealthy

Wealthy individuals use tax-efficient strategies to **legally** protect their money from taxes. One of these strategies is **Index Universal Life (IUL), which allows tax-free withdrawals in retirement.**

If you're saving for retirement, you need to consider:

- **How will taxes impact your withdrawals?**
- **Will tax rates go up by the time you retire?**
- **Are you using tax-free strategies like IUL?**

3. Healthcare Costs – The Biggest Expense in Retirement

Many retirees don't realize that **healthcare costs are one of the biggest expenses in retirement.** Medicare doesn't cover everything, and private insurance can be expensive.

The Hard Facts:

- A healthy **65-year-old couple retiring today** will need around **$315,000** just to cover medical expenses in retirement.
- **Long-term care (like nursing homes or in-home care)** can cost **$50,000 - $100,000 per year**—and Medicare doesn't cover it all.
- Medical expenses **increase faster than inflation,** meaning the cost will keep rising as you age.

Without proper planning, healthcare expenses **can wipe out your savings.**

The Bottom Line: Traditional Plans Are Not Enough

Most people enter retirement assuming **Social Security,** a **401(k), and some savings will be enough**. But **inflation,**

taxes, and healthcare costs can rapidly drain their funds, leaving them financially stressed.

So, what's the solution?

You need a **retirement strategy** that:

- **Protects your savings from inflation**
- **Provides tax-free income in retirement**
- **Allows you to access funds for healthcare without penalties**

This is why high-income earners use strategies like Index Universal Life (IUL) to build tax-free retirement wealth.

Chapter 2

UNDERSTANDING RETIREMENT PLANNING – WHAT ARE YOUR OPTIONS?

Planning for retirement requires understanding the different financial tools available to you. Each option has its pros and cons, and selecting the right mix will determine whether you retire stress-free or struggle financially. In this chapter, we'll explore the most common retirement vehicles, their benefits, limitations, and how they compare to alternative solutions like **Index Universal Life (IUL).**

---

1. Social Security – A Safety Net, Not a Retirement Plan

Social Security was designed as a **supplemental income,** not a full retirement plan. Yet, many Americans rely heavily on it.

Key Facts:

- The average Social Security benefit in 2024 is about **$1,907 per month** ($22,884 per year).
- If you were making **$100,000 per year before retirement, Social Security will replace only about 30-40%** of your income.
- Social Security funds are expected to **deplete by 2035**, meaning future benefits may be reduced.

Bottom line: Social Security alone is **not enough** to sustain a comfortable retirement.

---

2. 401(k) and Traditional IRAs – Tax-Deferred, But Not Tax-Free

Most people are told to invest in **401(k)s and IRAs**, but they come with hidden risks.

How They Work:

- **401(k):** Offered by employers, contributions are **tax-deferred**, meaning you don't pay taxes upfront but will pay **when you withdraw** the money.
- **IRA (Individual Retirement Account):** A self-directed retirement account with similar tax deferral benefits.

Limitations:

- **Taxes upon withdrawal:** Every dollar you take out is **taxed as ordinary income.**
- **Market risks:** Your money is directly tied to the stock market, meaning a crash can significantly impact your savings.
- **Required Minimum Distributions (RMDs):** You **must** start withdrawing (and paying taxes) at **age 73**, whether you need the money or not.

Bottom line: 401(k)s and IRAs help grow wealth, but taxes and market risks can **erode** your retirement funds.

---

3. Roth IRA – Tax-Free Growth, But with Limits

A **Roth IRA** is an attractive option because **it allows for tax-free withdrawals** in retirement.

How It Works:

- You contribute money **after taxes**, but your savings grow **tax-free.**
- After age 59½, you can withdraw your money **without paying taxes.**

Limitations:

- **Income limits:** In 2024, you can't contribute if you make more than **$161,000 (single) or $240,000 (married).**
- **Contribution cap:** The maximum annual contribution is **$7,000** ($8,000 if over 50).
- **Market risks:** Like a 401(k), your Roth IRA is still invested in stocks, meaning losses are possible.

Bottom line: The Roth IRA is great for tax-free income, but contribution limits make it hard to build **substantial** retirement wealth.

---

4. Annuities – Guaranteed Income, But with Restrictions

Annuities provide **guaranteed lifetime income**, but they are often misunderstood.

How They Work:

- You pay a lump sum or periodic payments to an insurance company.
- The insurer guarantees payments for life or a set period.

Limitations

- **Lack of flexibility:** Money is locked up, and early withdrawals result in **penalties.**
- **Tax implications:** Earnings are taxed as **ordinary income** upon withdrawal.

Bottom line: Annuities provide stability but often come with high fees and tax consequences.

---

5. Index Universal Life (IUL) – The Wealthy's Secret Retirement Strategy

IUL is a unique financial tool that allows for tax-free growth, protection against market losses, and flexible income in retirement.

How It Works:

- Your money grows **based on stock market performance**, but it's **protected from losses** with a **0% floor** (you never lose money in a downturn).
- Gains are locked in **tax-free**, and you can **withdraw money tax-free** using loans.
- There are **no contribution limits**, making it ideal for high-income earners.

Why It's a Game-Changer:

- **Tax-free income:** Unlike 401(k)s and traditional IRAs, IUL withdrawals are **not taxed.**
- **No market risk:** Your money grows with the market but is protected from crashes.
- **No contribution limits:** Unlike Roth IRAs, you can save **as much as you want.**
- **Built-in life insurance:** Provides a death benefit for your family.

Bottom line: IUL is one of the best-kept secrets of **the wealthy**, offering **tax-free growth, market protection, and financial flexibility.**

Choosing the Right Retirement Strategy

Each retirement tool has its place, but not all are created equal. Here's a quick **comparison**:

Retirement Tool	Tax-Free Growth?	Market Protection?	Contribution Limits?	Flexibility?
Social Security	No	Yes	N/A	No
401(k)/IRA	No (Tax-Deferred)	No	Yes	No

Retirement Tool	**Tax-Free Growth?**	**Market Protection?**	**Contribution Limits?**	**Flexibility?**
Roth IRA	Yes	No	Yes	No
Annuities	No	Yes	No	No
IUL	Yes	Yes	No	Yes

Final Thoughts: The Power of Proper Planning

Retirement planning isn't just about saving—it's about **saving wisely**. The wealthy don't rely on traditional methods alone. Instead, they use **tax-efficient, market-protected strategies like IUL** to build lasting wealth.

Chapter 3

WHAT IS AN INDEX UNIVERSAL LIFE (IUL) POLICY?

Understanding IUL: More Than Just Life Insurance

Most people think of life insurance as something that only benefits their loved ones when they pass away. However, **Index Universal Life (IUL) is much more than just life insurance**—it's a powerful financial tool that can help you build wealth, grow tax-free income, and create a stress-free retirement.

In this chapter, we will break down the **core concept of IUL**, how it differs from traditional life insurance, and why it has become a go-to **wealth-building strategy for high-income earners and smart investors.**

---

1. What is an IUL?

An **Index Universal Life (IUL) policy** is a type of **permanent life insurance** that includes a **cash value component** tied to the performance of a stock market index, like the **S&P 500 or Nasdaq**. Unlike traditional life insurance, which only provides a **death benefit**, an IUL allows you to:

- Grow your money tax-free
- Access your money tax-free in retirement
- Protect your money from stock market crashes
- Pass down wealth to your family tax-free

With an IUL, you get **both life insurance and an investment-like account** that grows over time without the risks of the stock market.

---

2. How is IUL Different from Traditional Life Insurance?

There are three main types of life insurance:

1. Term Life Insurance – The "Renting" Option

- Provides coverage for a **specific period** (10, 20, or 30 years).
- If you **outlive the term, the policy expires**—no cash value, no benefits.

- **Cheapest option**, but you get **no return on your money.**

2. Whole Life Insurance – The "Guaranteed" Option

- Coverage lasts **for life**, as long as you pay premiums.
- Builds **cash value**, but with **low returns (3-5% on average).**
- **Expensive premiums** with **limited flexibility**.

3. Index Universal Life (IUL) – The "Wealth-Building" Option

- **Permanent coverage** that never expires as long as premiums are paid.
- **Cash value grows tax-free**, linked to market performance but **protected from losses.**
- Offers **flexibility** in premium payments and withdrawals.
- Used by the wealthy as a **tax-free retirement tool.**

---

3. How an IUL Works: Growth Without the Risk

One of the biggest advantages of an IUL is how it grows money over time while protecting you from market downturns.

Growth is Based on a Stock Market Index

- Your money is not **invested** in the stock market. Instead, it is **linked to an index**, such as:
    - **S&P 500** (Tracks the 500 largest U.S. companies)
    - **Nasdaq 100** (Tracks tech companies like Apple, Google, Amazon)
- When the index goes up, your cash value grows.

You Are Protected from Market Crashes

- Unlike a 401(k) or Roth IRA, an IUL **has a 0% floor**—this means:
    - If the market **goes up**, you earn money.
    - If the market **crashes**, you lose **nothing** (your principal is protected).

Tax-Free Withdrawals Through Policy Loans

- Instead of withdrawing money and paying taxes (like with a 401(k)), you can take **tax-free loans** from your policy.

- The money continues to **grow** even when you borrow against it.
- You **never have to pay it back** if structured correctly, making it a powerful tax-free retirement strategy.

---

4. Why High-Income Earners Use IUL

Tax-Free Retirement Income – Unlike 401(k)s and traditional IRAs, IUL withdrawals **aren't taxed.**

No Contribution Limits – Unlike Roth IRAs, you can put in **as much money as you want.**

Market Protection – You get **stock market gains** without the risk of losing money.

Legacy & Wealth Transfer – Pass money **tax-free** to your family.

Example: A 40-year-old business owner puts $1,000 per month into an IUL. By age 65, they could have over **$1 million in tax-free cash value** and **a death benefit for their family**—all while **never worrying about stock market crashes.**

---

5. Is an IUL Right for You?

An IUL is a **powerful wealth-building tool**, but it's not for everyone. It works best for:

- High-income earners who want tax-free retirement savings.
- Business owners who want protection and flexibility.
- Anyone looking to protect wealth while growing it safely.
- People who want to leave a tax-free legacy for their family.

However, if you are **looking for quick returns** or have **a very limited budget**, a different strategy may be better.

6. How an IUL Builds Cash Value Tax-Free

One of the most powerful features of an **Index Universal Life (IUL) policy** is its ability to **grow cash value tax-free** while protecting your money from market downturns.

How Does the Cash Value Grow?

An IUL policy has a **cash value component** that earns interest based on the performance of a stock market index, such as:

- **S&P 500** – Tracks the 500 largest U.S. companies.
- **Nasdaq 100** – Focuses on tech giants like Apple, Amazon, and Google.

Unlike direct stock market investments, an IUL uses **index crediting**, meaning:

- When the market goes up, your cash value earns interest.
- When the market goes down, your cash value is **protected** (you never lose money).

This safety feature is possible because IULs have a **0% floor,** ensuring your money is never directly exposed to market losses.

Tax-Free Growth & Withdrawals

The cash value in an IUL grows **tax-free** under IRS rules, meaning you won't owe taxes on the money as it accumulates.

- No capital gains tax on growth.
- No income tax when you take out policy loans.
- No penalties for withdrawing funds at any age.

This makes IUL a great alternative to traditional retirement accounts like **401(k)s and IRAs**, which are subject to income taxes and penalties for early withdrawals.

---

7. IUL vs. Roth IRA: Key Differences

Both **IULs and Roth IRAs** allow tax-free withdrawals, but there are major differences that make IUL the **better choice for high-income earners.**

Features	Index Universal Life (IUL)	Roth IRA
Tax-Free Growth	Yes	Yes
Tax-Free Withdrawals	Yes	Yes (After Age 59½)
Contribution Limits	No Limits	Limited to $7,000/year ($8,000 if 50+)
Income Restrictions	None	Cannot contribute if income is too high ($161,000 single / $240,000 married in 2024)
Market Risk	No – 0% Floor Protection	Yes – Can Lose Money
Access to Cash	Anytime via Policy Loans	Locked Until Age 59½ (or penalties apply)
Death Benefit	Yes – Tax-Free Payout to Beneficiaries	No Death Benefit

Key Takeaways:

- IUL has NO contribution limits, while Roth IRAs limit how much you can invest each year.
- IUL is available to ALL income levels, while Roth IRAs restrict high earners from contributing.
- IUL offers a death benefit, making it a legacy-building tool, while Roth IRAs do not.
- IUL lets you access your money at any time, while Roth IRA withdrawals before age 59½ come with penalties.

For **high-income earners** and **business owners**, an IUL is often a **superior option** due to its **unlimited contributions and tax-free income potential.**

---

8. IRS Codes That Make IUL a Powerful Financial Tool

The tax advantages of an IUL are possible because of **specific IRS codes** that govern life insurance policies. Here are the key tax laws that make an IUL so powerful:

IRC 7702 – Tax Advantages of Life Insurance

IRC (Internal Revenue Code) **7702 defines life insurance** and ensures that:

- The cash value grows tax-free.
- The death benefit is tax-free for beneficiaries.
- Policyholders can access their cash value tax-free through policy loans.

This makes life insurance an ideal tool for **tax-free wealth accumulation and transfer.**

IRC 72(e) – Tax-Free Policy Loans

Under **IRC 72(e),** money taken from an IUL as a **loan** is **not taxable income.**

- **You can borrow against your cash value** without triggering taxes.
- **The money continues to grow** even while you borrow from it.
- **There's no required repayment**, as the death benefit can cover the loan balance.

This allows IUL owners to create **tax-free retirement income**, unlike traditional retirement accounts that are taxed upon withdrawal.

IRC 101(a) – Tax-Free Death Benefit

IRC **101(a) states that life insurance death benefits are tax-free** for beneficiaries.

- Your family receives the full payout without paying federal income tax.
- The wealth transfer is immediate, avoiding probate or delays.
- You can structure it to provide lifetime income for your heirs.

This ensures that your loved ones **inherit wealth tax-free,** making IUL a **powerful legacy-building tool.**

Final Thoughts: Why IUL is a Smart Retirement Strategy

An **Index Universal Life (IUL) policy** is **not just life insurance**—it's a **tax-free wealth-building tool** that helps:

Grow your money safely with market-linked returns and no risk of loss.

Access your savings tax-free whenever you need it.

Retire without worrying about taxes eating into your income.

Pass down wealth tax-free to your family.

While traditional retirement plans like **401(k)s and Roth IRAs** have **limits, restrictions, and tax risks**, an IUL provides:

- Unlimited contributions
- Tax-free withdrawals anytime
- Market protection with a 0% floor
- A guaranteed death benefit for your heirs

9. IUL – The Swiss Army Knife of Financial Planning

An **Index Universal Life (IUL) policy** is often referred to as the **"Swiss Army Knife"** of financial planning because it offers **multiple financial benefits** in one package. Just like a Swiss Army Knife has different tools for different needs, an IUL can be used for:

Retirement Planning – Tax-free income in your golden years.

College Funding – Helping your kids graduate debt-free.

Emergency Fund – Accessible savings for unexpected costs.

Wealth Transfer – Passing down money to your family tax-free.

Business Protection – A financial safety net for entrepreneurs.

Instead of using multiple financial products, **one IUL policy** can serve **multiple purposes,** making it a **versatile and powerful wealth-building tool.**

---

10. Using IUL for Retirement Planning

For most people, saving for retirement is a major financial goal. The problem? **Traditional retirement plans come with risks and restrictions:**

401(k)s and IRAs are taxed at withdrawal – You have no control over future tax rates.

Stock market downturns can wipe out years of savings.

Required Minimum Distributions (RMDs) force you to take money out at age 73, even if you don't need it.

How an IUL Solves These Problems

- Tax-Free Retirement Income – Withdrawals through policy loans are NOT taxed.
- Market Protection – You NEVER lose money due to market crashes (0% floor).
- No Contribution Limits – You can save as much as you want.
- No Age Restrictions – Access your money at ANY time, without penalties.

- Guaranteed Legacy – Your family gets a tax-free death benefit.

An IUL allows you to build **a private, tax-free retirement plan** that puts YOU in control—not the government.

---

11. Using IUL for College Planning

College tuition costs are rising every year, and many parents want a **smart way to save** for their children's education without being limited by traditional plans like **529 accounts.**

Problems with 529 Plans:

Funds must be used for education – If your child doesn't go to college, you pay a penalty.

Limited investment options – You don't control how your money grows.

Reduces financial aid eligibility – Money in a 529 counts against you when applying for aid.

Why an IUL is a Better College Savings Plan

- Money Can Be Used for Anything – College, starting a business, buying a home, etc.

- Tax-Free Growth & Withdrawals – Just like a Roth IRA, but with NO income limits.
- No Impact on Financial Aid – Since it's a life insurance policy, it's not counted as an asset.
- Continued Growth – Even if you borrow against the policy, the cash value keeps growing.

With an IUL, parents can build a **flexible, tax-free college fund** that doesn't limit their child's future options.

---

12. Using IUL as an Emergency Fund

Most financial experts recommend having **3 to 6 months of living expenses** saved in an emergency fund. The problem?

Savings accounts earn almost no interest.

CDs and bonds tie up your money.

With an IUL, you can **store your emergency savings** in a place that:

- Grows tax-free over time.
- Is accessible anytime via policy loans.
- Protects your money from market downturns.

Instead of keeping money in a **low-interest savings account**, an IUL allows you to **grow and access your emergency fund** at the same time.

---

13. Using IUL for Wealth Transfer & Legacy Planning

One of the biggest advantages of an IUL is its **tax-free death benefit.**

Traditional assets (stocks, real estate, 401(k)s) are taxed when passed down.

IUL provides a tax-free inheritance that avoids probate and estate taxes.

Your heirs get a guaranteed payout, no matter what happens in the market.

How Families Use IUL for Legacy Planning:

- Leave a tax-free inheritance to children and grandchildren.
- Create generational wealth without estate tax burdens.
- Protect family assets from probate and legal disputes.

With an IUL, you can ensure that **your loved ones are financially secure** long after you're gone.

---

14. Using IUL for Business Protection & Funding

For **entrepreneurs and business owners**, an IUL can be a **game-changing financial tool.**

Ways Business Owners Use IUL:

- Tax-Free Retirement Fund – Unlike a 401(k), an IUL has no contribution limits.
- Key Person Insurance – Protects the business if a key employee or owner dies.
- Business Loan Collateral – Lenders often accept an IUL as an asset.
- Tax-Free Business Buyout – Can fund a partner's buyout in case of retirement or death.

Many business owners use **IUL as their private bank,** allowing them to **borrow from their policy to fund business expenses** while still growing their wealth.

How an IUL Protects Your Money Against Garnishment, Lawsuits, and Divorce

One of the **lesser-known benefits** of an **Index Universal Life (IUL) policy** is that it offers **legal and financial protection** in ways that traditional savings accounts, 401(k)s, and even real estate cannot. In today's world, **lawsuits, creditors, and divorces** can quickly drain a person's wealth. An IUL, however, can serve as a **financial shield**, keeping your money safe and secure.

IUL & Asset Protection – Keeping Creditors Away

If you ever face **financial hardship, debt collection, or legal action**, your **savings, investments, and income** can be seized by creditors. However, in many states, life insurance policies, including IULs, are **exempt from creditor claims and bankruptcy proceedings.**

How an IUL Protects You:

- Creditor Protection – In most states, life insurance cash value cannot be taken by creditors.
- Bankruptcy Protection – If you declare bankruptcy, your IUL cash value remains protected.
- Lawsuit Shield – If someone sues you, your IUL assets are generally off-limits.

Example:

Let's say you own a business, and an unexpected lawsuit forces you to pay a large settlement. If you had saved your money in a **bank account, investment portfolio, or real estate**, that money could be seized. But if your wealth is in an IUL, in many cases, creditors **cannot touch it.**

Important Note: Asset protection laws vary by state, so it's important to check the regulations where you live.

How IUL Protects You in a Divorce

Divorce is one of the biggest financial risks a person can face. Many people lose **half or more of their assets** in a divorce settlement. However, **an IUL policy offers unique protection** that can help you **preserve** your wealth.

Ways IUL Protects You in a Divorce:

- Keeps Wealth Separate – If an IUL is structured properly, the cash value can be considered separate property (not subject to division).
- Tax-Free Loans Stay With You – If you take loans from your IUL, they don't count as income or marital assets.
- Estate Planning Advantage – You can use an IUL to pass wealth to your children instead of risking it in a divorce.

Example:

Imagine you are a high-income earner, and you're going through a divorce. If you had **$500,000 in a 401(k), it would likely be split in half.** However, if that money was inside an **IUL policy**, the cash value **might be protected**, allowing you to keep more of your wealth.

Tip: The best way to ensure **maximum protection** is to set up your IUL properly before marriage and work with a financial professional.

IUL & Protection from Medicaid Spend-Down

As people age, **long-term care costs** become a major concern. Many retirees who don't plan properly end up **spending down their savings** to qualify for Medicaid. However, an **IUL policy can protect your wealth from Medicaid spend-down rules.**

How an IUL Helps with Long-Term Care & Medicaid Planning:

- Cash Value Does NOT Count as an Asset – In many cases, an IUL's cash value is not considered when determining Medicaid eligibility.
- Tax-Free Death Benefit for Family – Even if you need long-term care, the money in your IUL still goes to your loved ones.
- Accelerated Benefits – Many IULs come with long-term care riders that allow you to access your death benefit early to pay for medical expenses.

Example:

A retiree with $200,000 in a **savings account** would need to **spend that money before qualifying for Medicaid**. But if that same $200,000 was inside an **IUL**, it could be **protected**, ensuring that it goes to their heirs instead of being drained by medical bills.

---

17. IUL – Your Financial Safety Net in Any Situation

An **Index Universal Life policy is more than just life insurance**—it's a **financial fortress** that helps protect your money from:

✔ Market crashes

✔ Taxes

✔ Lawsuits & creditors

✔ Divorce settlements

✔ Medical costs & Medicaid spend-down

This is why high-income earners, business owners, and professionals use **IUL as their private financial safety net**. It's **not just about growing wealth—it's about protecting it.**

Chapter

4

THE POWER OF SAVING – BUILDING WEALTH FOR A SECURE FUTURE

Chapter Layout:

1. Introduction: Why Saving Money is Non-Negotiable

- The difference between people who **struggle financially** and those who **retire stress-free** often comes down to **how much they save and where they put their money.**
- Many people **underestimate** the importance of saving because they focus on **earning more instead of keeping more.**
- **Statistic:** According to a **Bankrate survey,** nearly **57% of Americans** cannot cover a **$1,000 emergency expense** with their savings.

2. The State of Saving in America – Alarming Statistics

- Most Americans are **not saving enough**, and many are living **paycheck to paycheck.**
- **Retirement Savings Crisis:**
    - A **2023 report from Vanguard** found that the **average 401(k) balance** for Americans aged 55-64 is only **$256,200**—far from what's needed to retire comfortably.
    - Studies suggest that retirees **need at least $1 million** to retire comfortably, yet only **12% of Americans** have that much saved.
- **Emergency Fund Struggles:**
    - **CNBC reports** that **70% of Americans** have **less than $5,000 in savings.**
    - A Federal Reserve study shows that **40% of Americans** would **struggle to pay an unexpected $400 expense.**

Why Saving Money Matters – The Big Picture

The Bible gives us **timeless wisdom** about handling money. One of the most important financial principles is **saving for the future.**

Proverbs 21:20 – *"The wise store up choice food and olive oil, but fools gulp theirs down."*

This verse reminds us that **wise people prepare for what's ahead**, while **foolish people spend everything they have** without thinking about tomorrow. Saving money is not just about having extra cash—it's about **building a strong foundation that will protect you when life's storms come.**

The Parable of the Two Builders – A Lesson in Financial Stability

In **Matthew 7:24-27**, Jesus tells the story of **two men building houses**:

- One man built his house on a **rock**—when the storms came, his house **stood firm.**
- The other man built his house on **sand**—when the storms came, his house **collapsed.**

This parable isn't just about faith—it's also a financial lesson!

Your financial foundation matters. If you build your life on **spending everything, relying on debt, and failing to save**, your finances will collapse when hard times come. But if you build on **saving, investing wisely, and preparing for the future**, you'll stand strong even in tough times.

Rainy Days Are Coming – Will You Be Ready?

Life is unpredictable. You **will** face unexpected financial storms:

- A job loss
- A medical emergency
- A recession or inflation spike
- Unexpected home or car repairs

The question is: **Will you be prepared when it happens?**

If you have savings, you'll have peace of mind. If you don't, you'll be scrambling to survive. **Your future self depends on the decisions you make today.**

Build Your Financial Rock Today

- Save at least 20% of your income.
- Set up an emergency fund with 6-12 months of expenses.
- Invest in assets that grow, like IUL, retirement accounts, and real estate.
- Live below your means so you always have extra.

Wise people prepare for the future. Fools wait for disaster to happen.

The choice is yours: **Will you build your financial house on rock or sand?**

Choose where to save wisely

When saving money, there are four essential factors to consider: **Growth, Safety, Security, and Tax Advantage.** Each plays a critical role in ensuring long-term financial success.

Growth determines how fast your money doubles and whether it keeps pace with inflation. If your savings aren't growing, you're actually losing purchasing power over time. The Rule of 72 is a simple way to measure this—by dividing 72 by your interest rate, you can estimate how long it will take for your money to double. Choosing a savings vehicle with strong growth potential is key to building wealth.

Safety ensures that your money is protected from market volatility and economic downturns. Many traditional investment vehicles expose your hard-earned money to risks that can lead to major losses. True financial security means having a strategy that allows your money to grow while safeguarding it from sudden crashes.

Security means your savings act as a financial defense, much like the Bible says, *"Money is a defense" (Ecclesiastes 7:12).* Life is unpredictable—if you suffer a stroke, heart attack, or receive a cancer diagnosis, your savings should be accessible to cover medical expenses and protect your family's well-being. Without a financial safety net, unexpected hardships can quickly turn into financial disasters.

Tax Advantage ensures that when the time comes to access your money, you aren't penalized by excessive taxes. Many traditional retirement accounts, like 401(k)s and IRAs, defer taxes, meaning you'll owe a significant percentage of your withdrawals to the IRS later in life. A truly effective financial strategy minimizes tax liabilities, allowing you to keep more of your money when you need it most.

A strong financial foundation must check all four boxes. If your savings plan lacks even one of these elements, you risk financial instability in the future. The key is to build wealth in a way that ensures long-term security, protection, and tax efficiency—because rainy days will come, and when they do, you'll want to be standing on solid financial ground, not sinking sand.

Deciding where to save

When it comes to saving money, people have several options, each with its advantages and disadvantages. However, when compared to **Index Universal Life (IUL)**, many of these traditional savings methods fall short in key areas like growth potential, safety, security, and tax advantages. Let's break down some common savings vehicles and their limitations.

1. Keeping Money in the Bank (Checking/Savings Accounts)

- **Pros:** Easy access, FDIC-insured (up to $250,000 per depositor), safe from market risks.
- **Cons:** Extremely low interest rates (often below 1%), meaning your money doesn't grow and loses value due to inflation. While your money is safe, it is not growing effectively.

How IUL compares: Unlike bank accounts, an IUL allows your money to grow with stock market gains (without the risk of losses) while also providing tax advantages and liquidity through policy loans.

2. Stashing Cash Under the Mattress

- **Pros:** Immediate access, no banking fees or restrictions.
- **Cons:** No interest, no growth, vulnerable to theft, fire, and inflation. Cash loses value over time.

How IUL compares: Keeping money under a mattress is the worst way to save, as inflation erodes its value. With an

IUL, your money is protected from inflation and earns compound interest over time.

3. Certificates of Deposit (CDs)

- **Pros:** Higher interest than savings accounts, FDIC-insured, low risk.
- **Cons:** Locked in for a fixed period (e.g., 1-5 years), penalties for early withdrawal, taxable interest earnings.

How IUL compares: CDs provide safety but lack flexibility. An IUL, on the other hand, allows you to access funds through tax-free policy loans while still benefiting from market-linked growth.

4. Real Estate

- **Pros:** Potential for appreciation, passive income from rentals, tangible asset.
- **Cons:** High upfront costs, maintenance expenses, market fluctuations, property taxes, not liquid (hard to access cash quickly).

How IUL compares: Real estate is a great long-term investment, but it lacks liquidity and comes with ongoing expenses. An IUL allows for tax-free withdrawals and provides financial flexibility without the risks and costs of real estate ownership.

5. 401(k) and Traditional IRA

- **Pros:** Employer match (for 401k), tax-deferred growth, disciplined saving for retirement.
- **Cons:** Limited investment choices, penalties for early withdrawals before 59½, subject to Required Minimum Distributions (RMDs) after age 73, taxable withdrawals in retirement.

How IUL compares: While a 401(k) offers tax-deferred growth, withdrawals are taxable. An IUL provides tax-free income in retirement with no RMDs, offering more flexibility and tax efficiency.

6. Roth IRA

- **Pros:** Tax-free growth and withdrawals, no RMDs, good for long-term savings.
- **Cons:** Contribution limits ($7,000 per year for those under 50 in 2024), income restrictions, market risk.

How IUL compares: A Roth IRA offers tax-free growth, but it has strict contribution limits. An IUL, however, allows for unlimited contributions (depending on policy structure) and provides additional benefits like living benefits and tax-free policy loans.

Final Thoughts

Each savings vehicle has its place, but most lack the full combination of **growth, safety, security, and tax advantages that an IUL provides.** If you want **tax-free growth, protection from market downturns, liquidity, and a safety net in case of emergencies**, an IUL can be one of the best financial tools for building and protecting wealth over time.

How Much Money Should You Be Saving?

Saving money isn't just about setting money aside; it's about having a strategy that aligns with your financial goals and future security. The amount you should be saving depends on your income, lifestyle, and long-term objectives, but here are some proven methods to help you determine the right savings target for you.

1. The 50/30/20 Budgeting Rule

A simple yet effective method for managing your income is the **50/30/20 rule**, which divides your after-tax income into three categories:

- **50% Needs** – Essentials like rent, mortgage, utilities, groceries, and insurance.

- **30% Wants** – Entertainment, travel, dining out, and lifestyle expenses.
- **20% Savings & Debt Repayment** – Emergency funds, retirement accounts, and investments.

This method ensures a balanced approach to financial planning while prioritizing savings. However, if you want to build wealth faster, increasing the savings percentage can be beneficial.

2. Multiply Your Age by 10

Another effective rule is:

- Multiply your age by **10** to determine the minimum amount you should be saving per month.

For example:

- If you're **30 years old**, aim to save at least **$300 per month.**
- If you're **40 years old**, that number should increase to **$400 per month.**
- By **50**, you should be setting aside **at least $500 per month.**

This strategy ensures your savings grow as you get older and prepares you for a comfortable retirement.

3. The Pay Yourself First Method

Instead of saving what's left after expenses, this method suggests **saving first, then spending what's left.**

- Set up **automatic savings** each time you receive a paycheck.
- Aiming to save **at least 20-30%** of your income can significantly impact long-term financial security.

4. The 3-Month & 6-Month Emergency Fund Rule

Everyone should have an emergency fund covering at least **3 to 6 months of living expenses** in case of unexpected events like job loss, medical emergencies, or major car repairs.

- If your monthly expenses are **$3,000**, you should aim to have **$9,000 to $18,000** saved.
- This fund should be kept in a **high-yield savings account** for easy access.

Final Thoughts

The key to financial success is **consistency and discipline.** Whether you follow the **50/30/20 rule, multiply your age by 10, or pay yourself first**, the most important thing is to start **saving now** and adjust your strategy as your income and expenses change. **The more you save today, the more financial freedom you'll have in the future.**

The Role of Tithing in Financial Success

If you find yourself unable to save enough in your IUL to retire comfortably, there are three key areas to evaluate: **your lifestyle, your skillset, and your spirituality**. Each of these factors plays a crucial role in determining your financial future.

1. Your Lifestyle – Are You Living Above Your Means?

Many people struggle to save because they spend beyond their capacity. Financial security isn't just about how much you earn but how well you **manage** what you have. Take a close look at your expenses—are you prioritizing savings, or are luxuries taking up too much of your income? Downsizing unnecessary spending can free up more money to invest in your future.

2. Your Skillset – Do You Have the Skills to Pay the Bills?

Your ability to generate income directly impacts your financial growth. If your current income isn't enough to fund your retirement goals, consider **developing new skills** or exploring additional income streams. The most successful people continuously **invest in their own**

growth, learning new trades, starting side businesses, or enhancing their careers to increase their earnings.

3. Your Spirituality – Are You Honoring God with Your Finances?

Tithing is not just about giving; it's about **faith, discipline, and trust** in the One who provides. The Bible reminds us in **Deuteronomy 8:18**, *"Remember the Lord your God, for it is He who gives you the ability to produce wealth."* Tithing acknowledges that God is the source of your success and opens doors for financial wisdom and blessings.

Many people question whether they can afford to tithe, but the real question is: **Can you afford not to?** The principle of giving **first** and trusting that provision will follow is a mindset shift that has transformed countless lives.

We Are More Spiritual Than Physical

Money is not just numbers in a bank account; it carries **spiritual weight.** How you handle it reflects your mindset, your discipline, and your values. If you only focus on the physical—chasing money without purpose—you may find yourself constantly struggling. But when you align your **finances with principles of faith, wisdom, and discipline,** you create a foundation for lasting financial success.

As you build your wealth, **always remember the Source.** Financial success is not just about numbers; it's about stewardship, faith, and making choices that align with a greater purpose.

Here's a side-by-side breakdown of a budget for someone making $5,000 per month. The first column represents a budget where too much is spent on unnecessary expenses, while the second column shows a corrected version with better spending habits to save more money.

Unoptimized Budget – Spending Too Much

- **Rent/Mortgage:** $1,800
- **Car Payment:** $700
- **Auto Insurance:** $250
- **Groceries:** $600
- **Dining Out:** $500
- **Entertainment (Streaming, Movies, Subscriptions, etc.):** $300
- **Shopping (Clothes, Electronics, etc.):** $400
- **Utilities (Electricity, Water, Internet, Phone):** $350
- **Miscellaneous Spending:** $400

- **Savings & Investments:** $0

Total Expenses: $5,300 (Overspending by $300)

Optimized Budget – Smart Spending & Saving More

- **Rent/Mortgage:** $1,800 (No change, but could consider downsizing)
- **Car Payment: $400** (Bought a reliable used car instead of an expensive one)
- **Auto Insurance: $150** (Shopped for better rates)
- **Groceries: $400** (Meal planning and cutting unnecessary items)
- **Dining Out: $200** (Cooking at home more often)
- **Entertainment (Streaming, Movies, Subscriptions, etc.): $100** (Cutting unnecessary subscriptions)
- **Shopping (Clothes, Electronics, etc.): $150** (Less impulse buying)
- **Utilities (Electricity, Water, Internet, Phone): $300** (Negotiated bills, switched to budget-friendly options)

- **Miscellaneous Spending: $200** (Less unnecessary spending)
- **Savings & Investments (IUL, 401(k), Emergency Fund, etc.): $1,300**

Total Expenses: $5,000 (Now saving $1,300/month)

Key Takeaways:

- Cutting unnecessary spending (expensive car, dining out, shopping, entertainment) allows for more savings.
- By reallocating funds, this person can now invest in their IUL policy and other wealth-building strategies without needing additional income.
- Small changes in spending habits make a huge difference in financial security.

Chapter 5

TAX-FREE RETIREMENT – HOW THE WEALTHY USE IUL TO WIN

How Tax-Free Income Works with an IUL

One of the most powerful benefits of an **Index Universal Life (IUL) policy** is its ability to provide **tax-free retirement income.** Unlike traditional retirement accounts, such as 401(k)s and IRAs, which are taxed upon withdrawal, an IUL allows policyholders to access their money without being penalized by taxes. This tax-free advantage is what makes IUL a **favorite strategy among the wealthy** for building and protecting wealth.

1. The Power of Tax-Free Growth

When you put money into a 401(k) or a traditional IRA, your contributions are tax-deferred, meaning you

postpone paying taxes until you withdraw the money. However, when retirement comes, you could be in a higher tax bracket, and those withdrawals could cost you **thousands in taxes.**

With an IUL, your money grows **tax-free** within the policy. Thanks to **IRS Code 7702**, cash value inside a life insurance policy is not considered taxable income as long as it remains within the policy. This means your money compounds over time **without being eaten away by taxes.**

2. Accessing Your Money Without Taxes

Unlike traditional retirement plans that trigger **required minimum distributions (RMDs)** and taxes upon withdrawal, an IUL allows you to access your money **tax-free** through **policy loans.** Under **IRS Code 72(e),** policyholders can take loans against their cash value **without incurring taxes,** as long as the policy remains in force. The best part? These loans **do not need to be repaid** during your lifetime, as the death benefit will cover the outstanding loan balance.

3. Avoiding Tax Brackets in Retirement

Most retirees are shocked to learn that **Social Security income can be taxed** if they earn above a certain threshold. Traditional retirement plans like 401(k)s and IRAs add to your **taxable income**, pushing you into a **higher tax bracket** and causing more of your Social Security to be taxed.

An IUL solves this problem because policy loans **do not count as taxable income.** This allows you to supplement your retirement income **without increasing your tax burden**, keeping you in a lower tax bracket and ensuring you retain more of your hard-earned money.

4. The Wealthy Play the Tax-Free Game – Why Aren't You?

The wealthy understand the **tax code** and use it to their advantage. They strategically use IULs to:

- Build wealth **tax-free**
- Access money in retirement **without paying income tax**
- Protect their assets from market crashes
- Pass down wealth **tax-free** to their heirs under IRS Code 101(a)

5. Comparing IUL to Other Retirement Accounts

Let's break down the tax advantages of an IUL compared to other retirement accounts:

Retirement Plan	**Tax on Contributions**	**Tax on Growth**	**Tax on Withdrawals**
401(k) / IRA	Pre-Tax	Tax-Deferred	**Taxed**
Roth IRA	After-Tax	Tax-Free	Tax-Free
IUL	After-Tax	**Tax-Free**	**Tax-Free** (via loans)

6. The IRS Wants a Cut – But You Have a Choice

Traditional retirement accounts were **designed by the government**—which means they come with **rules that benefit the IRS** more than they benefit you. If you want **full control** over your money and want to **legally avoid unnecessary taxes**, an IUL is one of the most powerful financial vehicles available

How Tax-Free Income Works with an IUL: The Rules, The Science, and The History

The Concept of Tax-Free Growth in an IUL

An **Index Universal Life (IUL) policy** is a unique financial vehicle that allows your money to grow **tax-free**, be accessed **tax-free**, and be passed down to your beneficiaries **tax-free**. This advantage is possible due to specific sections of the U.S. **Internal Revenue Code (IRC)** that define how life insurance policies are taxed.

Unlike traditional retirement accounts (such as 401(k)s and IRAs), which are subject to **income taxes** upon withdrawal, an IUL offers tax-free benefits because the IRS classifies it as a **life insurance contract**, not a typical investment account.

The Tax Rules That Make IUL Tax-Free

Three key IRS codes make this possible:

1. **IRC 7702 – Tax-Advantaged Growth**
   - This section of the IRS tax code defines what qualifies as a **life insurance policy.**
   - As long as the policy meets certain guidelines, the **cash value inside an IUL grows tax-free.**
2. **IRC 72(e) – Tax-Free Withdrawals via Loans**
   - Normally, if you withdraw money from a 401(k) or IRA before age 59½, you pay **income tax** and a **10% early withdrawal penalty.**
   - With an IUL, you can access your cash value **without paying taxes** by using a policy loan.

3. **IRC 101(a) – Tax-Free Death Benefit**
   - Upon the policyholder's passing, the death benefit is paid out **100% tax-free** to beneficiaries.
   - This ensures that wealth is passed down efficiently, without government interference.

The Science Behind How the Loan Works in an IUL

Instead of withdrawing your money like a 401(k) or savings account, an IUL allows you to take a **loan against the cash value**. This is **not taxable** because you're not technically withdrawing your own money—you're borrowing from the insurance company while your cash continues to grow.

Here's how it works:

1. **Your Cash Value Acts as Collateral**
   - When you take a loan, the insurance company **does not touch your cash value**. Instead, they use it as **collateral** and lend you money from their own reserves.
   - This allows your **full cash value to continue growing**, even while you use the loaned funds.

2. **Interest Is Charged, But It's a Net Zero Loan**

    - The insurance company charges **interest** on the loan—typically **4% to 6%.**
    - However, the cash value in your IUL continues earning interest at a rate of **5% to 8%** (depending on market performance and policy structure).

→ If your cash value grows at the same or a higher rate than the loan interest, you end up paying nothing out of pocket—this is why it's called a Net Zero Loan.

3. **No Mandatory Repayment**

    - Unlike traditional loans, an IUL loan **does not require monthly payments.**
    - The loan balance is simply deducted from the **death benefit** when the policyholder passes away.

Why is it Called a Net Zero Loan?

A **Net Zero Loan** means that the interest you are paying is **offset by the growth of your policy's cash value.** If structured correctly, the money you borrow can be repaid

entirely by the continued growth of your policy—meaning you never actually "lose" any of your own money.

Example of a Net Zero Loan in Action:

- You take a **$100,000 loan** from your IUL.
- The insurance company charges **5% loan interest** = $5,000 per year.
- Your IUL's cash value is earning **7% interest** = $7,000 per year.
- Your policy **grows faster than the loan interest**, effectively making it a **net zero cost loan.**

Why the Wealthy Use IUL Loans Instead of Traditional Bank Loans

1. **No Credit Check or Approval Needed**
    - Unlike banks, insurance companies do not require **income verification** or a **credit check** to issue an IUL loan.
2. **No Mandatory Repayments**
    - Banks require monthly payments; IUL loans do not.

    - The loan balance is simply deducted from the **cash value** when the policyholder passes away.

3. **Tax-Free Access to Money**
    - Taking a loan from your 401(k) or IRA creates a **tax liability**—an IUL loan does not.

The History Behind Tax-Free IULs

The concept of using **life insurance as a tax-free wealth-building tool** has been around for over 100 years. The **Rockefellers, Vanderbilts, and other wealthy families** have used IULs and whole life insurance for **generations** to pass down wealth and create family legacies.

In the 1980s, the **IRS introduced laws (IRC 7702 & 72(e))** that established strict guidelines for tax-free life insurance policies. These laws are what allow modern **IULs to grow cash value tax-free** and provide **tax-free loans.**

The Bottom Line: Why You Should Use an IUL for Tax-Free Wealth

- **You can access your money tax-free** with policy loans.

- **Your cash value keeps growing even when you take a loan** (Net Zero Loan).
- **You never have to repay the loan out of pocket**—it's deducted from your future death benefit.
- **You legally avoid taxes** that would otherwise eat away at your retirement savings.
- **The wealthy have used this strategy for decades**—and now you can too.

How to Fund Your IUL for Maximum Growth

Funding your **Index Universal Life (IUL)** policy correctly is **crucial** to maximizing its benefits. There are two main ways to fund your IUL:

1. **Lump Sum Deposit** – A large, upfront contribution.
2. **Monthly (or Regular) Contributions** – Consistent smaller deposits over time.

Each method has its own advantages, and depending on your financial situation, you might use one or a combination of both.

Option 1: Lump Sum Deposit – Supercharging Your IUL Growth

A **lump sum** deposit means you put a **large amount of money** into your IUL at the very beginning. This strategy **accelerates** the policy's growth and allows you to start leveraging its benefits sooner.

Advantages of a Lump Sum Deposit:

- Immediate Growth Potential – Since the money is in the policy from day one, it can start earning compounded interest immediately.
- Maximizes Indexing Benefits – Your lump sum can participate in market growth right away, rather than waiting for monthly contributions to accumulate.
- Faster Access to Policy Loans – The more cash you have in your IUL, the sooner you can borrow against it tax-free for opportunities, emergencies, or retirement.
- Reduces the Risk of Policy Lapse – A well-funded policy is self-sustaining, meaning you're less likely to run into problems with policy fees or funding gaps.

Who Should Consider a Lump Sum?

- If you have **a large amount of cash sitting in a low-interest savings account**, transferring it into an IUL **protects it from taxes and market downturns.**
- If you've recently received **an inheritance, a work bonus, or sold an asset**, an IUL is a smart place to **park that money for tax-free growth.**

Option 2: Monthly (or Regular) Contributions – Building Over Time

If you don't have a large lump sum to invest, you can **fund your IUL gradually** by making **monthly, quarterly, or annual contributions.**

Advantages of Monthly Contributions:

- More Affordable for Most People – You don't need a huge amount of money upfront, making it accessible for individuals and business owners who prefer steady contributions.
- Dollar-Cost Averaging – If the market fluctuates, you're consistently adding funds over time, which can help balance out market highs and lows.

- Consistent Growth & Compounding – Even smaller contributions grow tax-free and provide long-term security.

Who Should Consider Monthly Contributions?

- If you want to **start your IUL now** but don't have a lump sum, regular deposits still allow you to build cash value steadily.
- If you have **consistent income**, setting up an automated contribution plan ensures your policy is always funded.

How to Maximize Your Growth – Best Practices

Max Fund Your Policy (Stay Below MEC Limits)

- The IRS sets a limit on how much money you can put into an IUL before it loses its **tax-free advantages.**
- Work with your advisor to make sure you are contributing **as much as possible without crossing the MEC (Modified Endowment Contract) threshold.**

Increase Contributions When Possible

- If you get a raise, a bonus, or extra income, consider increasing your IUL contributions. The more you put in, the more your cash value will grow **tax-free.**

Leverage Business or Side Income

- If you are a business owner or have side income, use **business profits** to fund your IUL as a **tax-advantaged strategy.**

Use Lump Sum + Monthly Contributions

- One of the best strategies is to **start with a lump sum** to kickstart growth, then continue **adding monthly payments** to keep compounding.

Final Thoughts: Which Option is Best for You?

Both lump sum deposits and monthly contributions are **effective ways to fund an IUL**, but the best strategy depends on:

Your Financial Situation – Do you have extra cash available now, or would you rather build over time?

Your Long-Term Goals – Are you looking for fast growth or steady, consistent funding?

Your Tax Strategy – How much do you want to protect from taxes immediately?

If you have money sitting in a bank, **a lump sum deposit** can **maximize your IUL's power immediately.** If you're looking to build over time, **monthly contributions still allow you to secure tax-free wealth.**

Either way, the key is **funding your IUL consistently and strategically** so that it can **work for you and your financial future.**

How the Rich Legally Avoid Taxes Using Life Insurance

One of the biggest financial secrets of the wealthy is that they don't just work hard for their money—they make sure their money **works for them, tax-free**. They use legal strategies, especially **Index Universal Life (IUL) policies,** to minimize their tax burden and maximize their wealth.

The **tax code** is designed to reward those who invest in certain financial vehicles, and life insurance happens to be one of them. Instead of putting all their money in traditional retirement accounts like 401(k)s and IRAs—which are subject to **future tax increases**—the wealthy put a significant portion into **cash-value life insurance**

policies, allowing them to grow and access their money **without paying taxes.**

Why Life Insurance is a Powerful Tax-Free Wealth Strategy

The IRS provides **special tax benefits** to life insurance under specific codes:

- IRC 7702 – Defines how life insurance policies qualify for tax advantages.
- IRC 72(e) – Allows tax-deferred cash value growth and tax-free access through loans.
- IRC 101(a) – Provides tax-free death benefits to beneficiaries.

The rich take advantage of these codes to create **tax-free income streams**, preserve generational wealth, and avoid taxes on capital gains.

How the Wealthy Use IULs to Avoid Taxes

Tax-Free Growth – Money inside an IUL grows tax-free, just like a **Roth IRA**, but without the **income limits.**

Tax-Free Withdrawals via Policy Loans – Instead of withdrawing from their account (which would be taxable), the wealthy take **policy loans** against their cash value. The IRS does not consider loans as **taxable income**, making this a **tax-free income source.**

No Required Minimum Distributions (RMDs) – Unlike traditional 401(k)s or IRAs, an IUL **doesn't force you to start withdrawing money at a certain age.** This allows for greater control over when and how you access your funds.

No Capital Gains Tax – Unlike real estate or stock investments, where profits can be taxed up to **20%**, money inside an IUL is protected from capital gains taxes.

This strategy allows high-income earners and business owners to **store wealth, borrow against it tax-free, and pass it down to their heirs without the government taking a large chunk.**

How Tax Brackets Affect Retirement Income

Many people assume they will be in a **lower tax bracket in retirement**, but this is not always the case.

Here's why:

□**Taxes Will Likely Be Higher in the Future** – With national debt increasing, many economists predict that tax rates **will rise** in the coming years.

2️⃣**Your Retirement Income May Be Higher Than You Think** – If you have a pension, Social Security, and withdrawals from a 401(k) or IRA, you may end up in a **higher tax bracket than expected.**

3️⃣**Taxation of Social Security** – Up to **85% of Social Security benefits can be taxed** depending on your income level.

Here's a breakdown of **2024 federal tax brackets:**

Taxable Income (Single Filers)	Tax Rate
Up to $11,000	10%
$11,001 - $44,725	12%
$44,726 - $95,375	22%
$95,376 - $182,100	24%
$182,101 - $231,250	32%
$231,251 - $578,125	35%
Over $578,126	37%

Taxable Income (Married, Filing Jointly)	Tax Rate
Up to $22,000	10%

Taxable Income (Married, Filing Jointly)	Tax Rate
$22,001 - $89,450	12%
$89,451 - $190,750	22%
$190,751 - $364,200	24%
$364,201 - $462,500	32%
$462,501 - $693,750	35%
Over $693,751	37%

Example:

- If a retired couple has **$100,000 in taxable income,** they will be taxed at **22% or higher**, meaning they may lose over **$20,000** to taxes every year!

How IUL Protects You from High Retirement Taxes

- **Tax-Free Retirement Income** – With an IUL, you avoid taxation on withdrawals because you're taking money through **policy loans**, which are not considered taxable income.

- **No Contribution Limits** – Unlike a Roth IRA, an IUL has **no annual contribution cap**, allowing you to put in as much money as you want.
- **Eliminates Social Security Taxation** – Since loans from an IUL don't count as income, they won't cause your **Social Security benefits to be taxed.**
- **Passes Wealth Tax-Free** – Your **heirs receive the death benefit tax-free**, ensuring your legacy isn't eaten up by the IRS.

Final Thoughts: Why You Should Follow the Wealthy

The rich don't rely on 401(k)s or IRA's alone because they understand that **taxes will eat away at their retirement savings**. Instead, they use **strategic tax-free vehicles like IULs** to protect and grow their wealth.

By incorporating an IUL into your financial plan, you're **legally avoiding unnecessary taxes, securing your future, and ensuring your retirement income remains untouched by tax hikes.**

If you don't have a strategy for **tax-free retirement**, you could be leaving **hundreds of thousands of dollars on the**

table—money that could have been working for you and your family instead.

How to Structure an IUL for Maximum Growth

A properly structured **Indexed Universal Life (IUL) policy** can be a **powerful wealth-building tool**, but **not all IULs are created equal.** Many people make the mistake of setting up their policy incorrectly, **leaving money on the table** instead of maximizing its full potential. In this section, we'll break down the **right way to design an IUL for retirement income**, how to **maximize cash accumulation**, and the **common mistakes to avoid.**

---

1. The Right Way to Design an IUL for Retirement Income

If your goal is to build **tax-free retirement income**, your IUL needs to be structured differently than a traditional life insurance policy focused solely on the death benefit. The key is to **prioritize cash value accumulation** while keeping costs low.

✓ **Lower the Death Benefit** – The larger the death benefit, the more money goes toward insurance costs instead of cash growth. Lowering the death benefit to the IRS minimum requirement ensures **more of your premium** goes toward cash accumulation.

✓ **Max-Fund the Policy** – Instead of just paying the minimum premium, **fund your IUL up to the IRS limit (MEC limit)** to maximize tax-free growth. This keeps costs low while compounding cash value faster.

✓ **Use an Increasing Death Benefit (Initially)** – This allows the policy to build cash value **without being classified as a Modified Endowment Contract (MEC)**, which would remove the tax-free benefits.

✓ **Choose the Right Indexing Strategy** – Most IULs let you choose **how your cash value grows**, often tied to indexes like the **S&P 500**. Understanding **cap rates, participation rates, and floors** is key to maximizing growth.

---

2. How to Maximize Cash Accumulation Instead of Just Focusing on the Death Benefit

Most people mistakenly focus **only on the death benefit** when purchasing life insurance. While protecting your family is important, the real **power of an IUL lies in its cash accumulation potential.**

Ways to Maximize Cash Value:

Overfund Your Policy – Pay more than the minimum premium to accelerate growth.

Utilize Policy Loans Strategically – Withdraw tax-free income without depleting your cash value.

Choose the Right Index Strategy – A higher **participation rate** or **uncapped options** allow for better gains.

Avoid High Fees – Ask about policy charges, as some IULs have **hidden fees** that eat into growth.

Example:

John funds his IUL with $1,500/month instead of just $500/month. By the time he retires, his cash value is **3x larger**, allowing him to withdraw **significantly more tax-free income** each year.

---

3. The Importance of Overfunding Your Policy

Overfunding your IUL is the single most powerful way to maximize your retirement income. By contributing as much as possible without triggering a **Modified Endowment Contract (MEC)**, you allow your **money to compound faster**.

✓ Why Overfund?

- Your cash value grows significantly faster.
- You can take **larger tax-free loans** in retirement.
- The policy becomes **self-sustaining**, meaning you won't have to keep paying premiums later in life.

Example:

Basic Funding: Contributing only the minimum might result in a **small** cash value after 20 years.

Overfunding: Maximizing contributions could **double or triple** the available retirement income.

---

4. Avoiding Common Mistakes People Make When Setting Up an IUL

Many people purchase an IUL **without fully understanding how it works**, leading to **disappointing results.** Here are the **biggest mistakes** to avoid:

Mistake #1: Underfunding the Policy

Problem: If you only pay the minimum, your cash value will grow **very slowly**, and the policy could become too expensive to maintain.

Solution: Always aim to **overfund** your IUL up to the **MEC limit** for maximum benefits.

Mistake #2: Choosing the Wrong Death Benefit Option

Problem: A level death benefit means **less cash accumulation** early on.

Solution: Use **an increasing death benefit** until your cash value grows, then switch to level.

Mistake #3: Not Understanding Fees & Caps

Problem: Some IULs have **low cap rates or high fees,** limiting growth.

Solution: Work with an experienced **financial professional** to select the **best IUL structure** for you.

Mistake #4: Treating an IUL Like a Short-Term Investment

Problem: IUL is **not a get-rich-quick plan**—it works best as a **long-term strategy.**

Solution: Plan to keep your policy for **at least 15-20 years** to see real benefits.

Conclusion: Set Up Your IUL the Right Way

A well-structured IUL **policy** is one of the most powerful ways to build **tax-free retirement income** while protecting your wealth. However, **how you set it up** determines how successful it will be

Chapter 6

DEMYSTIFYING LIFE INSURANCE – FROM TERM TO IUL

Life insurance has been around for centuries, evolving from a simple way to protect families into a **powerful financial tool** that can provide tax-free wealth, retirement income, and financial security. Many people misunderstand life insurance, assuming it's just about **a death benefit**—but in reality, it can be a **living benefit** that helps you **build wealth, protect assets, and create financial freedom.**

In this chapter, we'll **trace the history of life insurance**, explain the **differences between term and permanent insurance**, and reveal how **Index Universal Life (IUL)** became one of the most strategic financial tools available today.

A Brief History of Life Insurance

Life insurance dates back to **Ancient Rome**, where "burial clubs" helped families cover funeral expenses. But modern life insurance began in the **18th century** and has since evolved into the powerful industry we know today.

Key Milestones in Life Insurance History

- **1706** – The first life insurance company, **The Amicable Society**, was established in London.
- **1759** – The first life insurance company in the U.S., **The Presbyterian Ministers' Fund**, was founded in Pennsylvania.
- **1875** – The first mutual life insurance company, **The Widows and Orphans Benefit Fund**, was created to provide benefits for families.
- **1900s** – Term and whole life insurance became standard policies.
- **1970s-1980s** – Universal life insurance (UL) was introduced as a flexible alternative to whole life insurance.
- **1997** – **Indexed Universal Life (IUL) was created**, allowing policyholders to earn interest based on stock market performance without market risk.

Life insurance has **evolved from a simple safety net to a dynamic wealth-building tool**, offering benefits far beyond just a payout after death.

Term Life vs. Permanent Life Insurance – Understanding the Basics

The two main types of life insurance are **term life** and **permanent life insurance**. Let's break them down.

Feature	**Term Life Insurance**	**Permanent Life Insurance (Whole Life, UL, IUL)**
Coverage Duration	10, 20, or 30 years	Lifetime (as long as premiums are paid)
Cash Value?	No cash value	Builds cash value over time
Affordability	Lower initial cost	Higher initial cost, but builds value
Expires?	Yes	No, stays in force
Tax Benefits?	No	Tax-free growth, tax-free loans
Living Benefits?	No	Can access money while alive

Many people **start with term life insurance** because it's **cheaper**, but it **expires** after a certain period and provides no financial benefits beyond the death benefit. That's why the wealthy often choose **permanent life insurance**—especially **Indexed Universal Life (IUL)**—which allows them to **build tax-free wealth while maintaining protection.**

The Evolution of Universal Life Insurance – The Birth of IUL

Why Did Universal Life Insurance (UL) Emerge?

In the **1970s and 1980s,** interest rates were high, and people wanted **more flexibility in their life insurance policies.** Universal Life (UL) was created to offer:

- **Flexible premiums** (pay more or less when needed)
- **Adjustable death benefits** (increase or decrease coverage)
- **Cash value accumulation** (money grows over time)

However, traditional UL had a **problem**—its cash value was based on fixed interest rates, which could drop when economic conditions changed.

The Birth of Indexed Universal Life (IUL) – A Game Changer

In **1997, Indexed Universal Life (IUL)** was introduced to **solve the problem** of fluctuating interest rates. Instead of a **fixed** interest rate, IUL policies allow cash value to **grow based on stock market indexes** (like the S&P 500) while still guaranteeing **no market losses.**

This was revolutionary because it combined:

✓ **Stock market-like gains** (without the risk of losing money)

✓ **Tax-free growth and withdrawals** (unlike traditional investments)

✓ **Permanent life insurance protection** (never expires if funded properly)

IUL became **the go-to solution for high-income earners, business owners, and savvy investors** looking to build wealth **without worrying about market crashes or taxes.**

Life Insurance Statistics – Why It's More Important Than Ever

Here are some shocking statistics that highlight why life insurance is **essential:**

Only 52% of Americans have life insurance, and 40% of policyholders feel underinsured. *(LIMRA, 2023)*

1 in 3 families would face financial hardship within **one month** if the primary earner passed away. *(Life Happens, 2022)*

68% of people say they need life insurance, but many don't understand its benefits. *(LIMRA, 2023)*

The **average funeral costs $7,848**—yet 56% of Americans have less than **$1,000 in savings.** *(NFDA, 2023)*

These numbers show that many people **fail to plan for financial protection**—but those who do are setting themselves up for **long-term success.**

The Power of IUL – More Than Just Life Insurance

An IUL **policy isn't just about dying—it's about living.** It serves as:

- **Retirement Income** – Tax-free withdrawals can supplement retirement savings.
- **College Savings** – A tax-free alternative to 529 plans.
- **Emergency Fund** – Access cash without penalties.

- **Business Protection** – Helps fund buy-sell agreements and key-person policies.
- **Legacy Building** – Passes wealth to heirs tax-free.

Final Thoughts – Life Insurance Is an Asset, Not an Expense

Many people **avoid** life insurance because they think of it as an **expense** rather than an **asset**. But history shows that life insurance **has evolved into one of the most powerful financial tools available**—especially when structured as an IUL policy.

If you're looking for a **tax-free, risk-free way to build wealth, protect your family, and secure your retirement**, IUL is one of the **best-kept secrets of the wealthy.**

The question is: **Are you ready to take control of your financial future?**

Understanding Different Types of Life Insurance and Their Purpose

Life insurance is more than just financial protection—it's a tool that can be **strategically used** for different life events, financial planning, and legacy building. Let's break down the **four main types of life insurance** and what they are designed for.

---

1. Term Life Insurance – Protection for "Dying Too Soon"

Term life insurance is the **simplest and most affordable** form of life insurance. It provides coverage for a specific period, typically **10, 20, or 30 years.** If the insured person passes away within the term, their beneficiaries receive the **death benefit.** However, if they outlive the term, the policy **expires with no cash value.**

Who is it for?

- Young families who need affordable protection.
- Homeowners with a mortgage who want financial security for their family.
- Business owners who need coverage for key employees.

Example Use:

A 35-year-old father buys a **30-year term life policy** to ensure that if he dies before his children are financially independent, they will be taken care of.

⚠ **Downside:** Term insurance has **no cash value** and **expires**, meaning if you don't pass away during the term, you get nothing in return.

---

2. Final Expense Insurance – Covering Funeral & Burial Costs

Final expense insurance (also called **burial insurance**) is a **small whole life insurance policy** designed to cover **funeral costs, medical bills, and small debts.** The coverage amount typically ranges from **$5,000 to $50,000,** and it's **easier to qualify for**, even for seniors or those with health issues.

Who is it for?

- Seniors who don't want their family to struggle with funeral expenses.
- People with limited savings who want to avoid leaving financial burdens.

Example Use:

A 70-year-old grandmother purchases a **$25,000 final expense policy** so her family doesn't have to worry about paying for her funeral.

⚠ **Downside:** This policy is **not meant for wealth building**—it only covers end-of-life expenses.

---

3. Indexed Universal Life (IUL) – The Wealth-Building Strategy

Indexed Universal Life (**IUL**) is one of the **most powerful** life insurance options available today. It combines **permanent life insurance** with a **cash value account** that grows based on stock market performance **without risk of loss.**

Who is it for?

- People who want **tax-free** retirement income.
- Business owners and high-income earners who want **tax advantages.**
- Parents who want to build **wealth for their children.**

Example Uses:

- A 40-year-old entrepreneur funds an **IUL policy** to **grow tax-free wealth,** which he can later access for **retirement income.**
- A 35-year-old father sets up an IUL for his child's **college savings**—instead of a 529 plan, which limits how the money is used.

Downside: IUL **requires long-term funding** and discipline to maximize its benefits.

Transferring Wealth Instead of Debt

"A good man leaves an inheritance to his children's children." – Proverbs 13:22

One of the biggest financial mistakes people make is **transferring debt instead of wealth.** Many families leave behind **funeral expenses, unpaid loans, and financial struggles** rather than a financial legacy.

Instead of passing on **burdens,** you can use **life insurance to transfer generational wealth.**

✓ **IUL can be used to fund college education, buy a home, or start a business for your children.**

✓ **Whole life insurance can guarantee a lump sum payout for your heirs.**

✓ **Term insurance can protect your family during critical earning years.**

The **wealthy don't leave their families with bills—they leave them with assets.** The question is: **What will your financial legacy be?**

Who is Eligible for an Indexed Universal Life (IUL) Policy?

An **Indexed Universal Life (IUL) policy** is a financial tool designed for individuals looking to **build wealth, protect their family, and secure a tax-free retirement**. However, not everyone qualifies for an IUL. Eligibility is based on factors like **age, health, and financial ability** to maintain the policy.

1. Age Requirements

IUL policies are available for a wide range of ages, from **infants to seniors**. The **younger you are**, the lower the premium and the more time your cash value has to grow. Many parents set up IUL policies for their **children**, locking in **low costs and early wealth accumulation**.

2. Health Considerations

Since IUL is a life insurance policy, you must go through an **underwriting process** to determine eligibility. Insurance companies assess:

- **Medical history** – Pre-existing conditions can impact approval and pricing.
- **Current health status** – A medical exam may be required.

- **Family history** – Some hereditary conditions could affect eligibility.
- **Lifestyle choices** – High-risk activities (smoking, dangerous hobbies) may result in higher premiums or even denial.

Even if you have health challenges, some insurers offer **no-medical-exam IUL policies**, though they may come with **higher costs and lower benefits.**

3. Financial Qualification

IUL is not just about qualifying physically—it's also about having the **financial ability** to fund the policy. You must be able to:

- **Commit to regular contributions** (monthly or lump sum).
- **Choose a premium amount** that fits your budget without financial strain.
- **Understand the long-term nature** of the policy—this is a wealth-building tool, not a short-term fix.

4. Occupation & Lifestyle Risks

Some professions and hobbies are considered **high-risk,** which may impact eligibility or premiums. These include:

- **Military personnel or first responders**

- **Pilots or deep-sea divers**
- **Extreme sports athletes**
- **Frequent travelers to dangerous regions**

Insurance companies evaluate risk levels and may adjust coverage or costs accordingly.

Who Benefits Most from an IUL?

- **Young professionals** looking for tax-free retirement growth.
- **High-income earners** who want to shelter wealth from taxes.
- **Entrepreneurs** who need financial flexibility.
- **Parents** who want to set up **legacy wealth** for their children.
- **Anyone seeking protection** while growing cash value safely.

In short, almost anyone **can qualify for an IUL**—but the **sooner you start, the better your benefits** will be!

Chapter

7

HOW TO MANAGE YOUR IUL POLICY & MAKE ADJUSTMENTS

What Happens After You Set Up Your IUL?

Once you establish your **Indexed Universal Life (IUL) policy**, your financial journey with it is just beginning. Unlike traditional life insurance, an IUL is a **dynamic financial tool** that requires periodic management to ensure it continues working effectively for your long-term goals. Your cash value will grow over time, and depending on your needs, you may want to **adjust contributions, change investment strategies, or leverage policy loans.** Understanding how to manage and optimize your IUL can make a significant difference in maximizing its benefits.

Tracking Your Cash Value Growth Over Time

Your IUL's cash value grows based on the **performance of the market index** it is linked to. Unlike direct stock market investments, your IUL has a **floor**, meaning you will never lose money due to market downturns. However, tracking your policy's performance regularly will help you:

- See how much your cash value is growing.
- Determine whether adjustments are necessary.
- Ensure your contributions are aligned with your financial goals.

Most insurance companies provide **online portals or annual statements** that give you a breakdown of your policy's performance. Make it a habit to review these reports to stay informed about your policy's progress.

Can You Adjust Your Contributions?

One of the great advantages of an IUL is its **flexibility** in contributions. Life circumstances change, and your IUL allows you to adjust your premiums accordingly. Here's how:

- **Increase Contributions:** If you experience an increase in income or receive a financial windfall, you can contribute **more** to your IUL. This helps you maximize **cash accumulation** and future retirement income.

- **Decrease Contributions:** If you encounter financial difficulties, you can **reduce your premium payments** while keeping your policy active (as long as there is sufficient cash value to cover the cost of insurance).

This flexibility ensures that your IUL remains a **viable long-term financial asset**, even if your financial situation fluctuates.

What to Do If You Need to Pause Payments Due to Financial Hardship

Life is unpredictable, and there may be times when you cannot make your scheduled IUL premium payments. Unlike traditional term life insurance, where missing payments could result in losing coverage, an IUL provides options to help you maintain your policy:

1. **Utilize Your Cash Value:** If your policy has built up enough cash value, you can use it to **cover the cost of insurance** and keep the policy in force.

2. **Reduce Premiums Temporarily:** Work with your insurance provider to temporarily **lower your contributions** until you are financially stable again.
3. **Resume Payments When Ready:** Once your financial situation improves, you can **increase contributions** to continue building your cash value and maintaining your policy's effectiveness.

Being proactive and communicating with your insurance provider is key to managing temporary financial hardships while protecting your IUL policy.

Can You Change Your Index Strategy as the Market Shifts?

IUL policies allow you to allocate your cash value among different **index crediting strategies**. Some strategies provide **higher growth potential** but come with a capped return, while others offer **more stability**. You may want to:

- Shift to a more **aggressive strategy** during a strong market period.
- Move to a **conservative strategy** if the market is volatile.
- Utilize a **blend of strategies** to balance risk and reward.

Most insurance companies allow policyholders to adjust their index allocations **annually**, so staying informed about market trends and working with your financial advisor can help you make the best choices.

How to Use Policy Loans Wisely to Avoid Reducing Your Retirement Income

One of the **biggest benefits** of an IUL is the ability to **borrow against your cash value tax-free**. However, improper use of policy loans can reduce your future income. Here's how to use them wisely:

When to Consider Taking a Loan

- **Investment Opportunities:** If you have an opportunity to invest in a **business or real estate**, using a policy loan can be a smart way to fund it without disrupting your investment gains.
- **Emergency Expenses:** Instead of taking a traditional loan with high interest rates, you can **borrow from your IUL** to cover unexpected financial emergencies.
- **Supplementing Retirement Income:** A properly structured IUL can provide **tax-free income in retirement** through **policy loans**, allowing you to

maintain your lifestyle without increasing your taxable income.

How to Avoid Policy Loan Pitfalls

- **Pay the Interest:** Although the policy loan is tax-free, interest accrues over time. If not managed properly, this can **reduce your cash value and death benefit.**
- **Limit Borrowing to Necessary Amounts:** Borrowing too much from your policy can impact its performance and longevity. Only take what is needed and **leave enough to continue compounding growth.**
- **Work With a Professional:** Consulting with a financial advisor ensures you are using policy loans **strategically** without jeopardizing your financial future.

The Importance of Annual Reviews to Ensure Your Policy is Optimized

To get the **most out of your IUL**, schedule an **annual policy review** with your financial advisor or insurance provider. During this review, you should:

- **Check your cash value growth** and make sure it's on track with your goals.
- **Assess if you need to increase or decrease premiums** based on your financial situation.
- **Reevaluate your index strategy** to ensure you're maximizing returns.
- **Review your loan balance** if you have borrowed from your policy.
- **Update beneficiaries** if necessary.

Just like you visit a doctor for regular check-ups, your IUL needs consistent **monitoring and adjustments** to remain a strong financial tool.

Final Thoughts

Your IUL is not a "set it and forget it" policy—it requires **active management** to maximize its benefits. By tracking your cash value, adjusting contributions as needed, utilizing policy loans wisely, and conducting annual reviews, you can ensure that your IUL remains a **powerful financial asset** for years to come.

Whether you are **growing your wealth, preparing for retirement, or protecting your family**, properly managing your IUL will help you achieve financial security and peace of mind.

Chapter

8

THE INFINITE BANKING CONCEPT – BECOMING YOUR OWN BANK

What is Infinite Banking, and How Does It Work?

Infinite Banking is a financial strategy that allows individuals to take control of their own financing by using a specially structured Indexed Universal Life (IUL) policy. Instead of relying on traditional banks and lenders for loans, you use the cash value of your IUL to borrow money and pay yourself back, keeping the interest within your own financial ecosystem. This concept, made popular by Nelson Nash in his book *Becoming Your Own Banker*, enables individuals to use life insurance as a personal banking system.

The key to Infinite Banking is that money inside an IUL continues to grow with compound interest, even when you take a loan against it. This gives policyholders access to tax-free loans while maintaining the growth potential of their cash value. By leveraging this strategy, you can use your own funds for major purchases, investments, and emergency expenses without ever having to depend on traditional financial institutions.

How the Wealthy Use Life Insurance to Finance Major Purchases

The ultra-wealthy have been using life insurance as a financial tool for decades. Instead of depleting their assets or taking out traditional loans for large purchases, they borrow against their IUL policies to fund real estate, businesses, and even personal luxuries like cars and vacations. This allows them to keep their money growing while still having access to liquidity.

Unlike conventional loans, policy loans from an IUL do not require a credit check, do not impact your credit score, and do not have a mandatory repayment schedule. This financial flexibility enables individuals to make strategic financial moves while ensuring their money remains in a protected and tax-advantaged environment.

How to Borrow from Yourself and Pay Yourself Back Instead of a Bank

One of the core principles of Infinite Banking is the idea of "becoming your own bank." Here's how it works:

1. **Accumulate Cash Value** – By funding an IUL policy consistently, you build up cash value that earns interest and grows over time.

2. **Take Out a Loan** – When you need money, instead of going to a bank, you take a policy loan against your own cash value.

3. **Use the Funds** – You can use this money for anything: buying a car, funding a business, investing in real estate, or covering unexpected expenses.

4. **Pay Yourself Back with Interest** – Instead of repaying a bank, you make payments back to your policy, effectively replenishing your own wealth and keeping interest payments in your financial ecosystem.

By following this strategy, you position yourself as both the borrower and the lender, maximizing your financial efficiency and ensuring that your money works for you at all times.

The Power of Compounding Interest When Using an IUL for Financing

Albert Einstein once called compound interest "the eighth wonder of the world." When using an IUL policy for Infinite Banking, your money continues to earn compound interest even when you take out loans. This is because you are not actually withdrawing money; you are borrowing against your policy while your cash value remains intact and continues to grow.

Unlike traditional bank loans, where interest payments go to financial institutions, an IUL loan ensures that interest payments remain within your policy, strengthening your long-term financial position. Over time, this allows you to build wealth exponentially, rather than losing money to external lenders.

Using IUL to Fund Real Estate, Business Ventures, and College Tuition

One of the biggest advantages of Infinite Banking is the ability to leverage your IUL policy to fund major investments. Here's how it works for different financial needs:

- **Real Estate** – Instead of taking out a mortgage or hard money loan, you can use your IUL policy to finance down payments or purchase properties outright. You then pay yourself back using rental income or other revenue streams.
- **Business Ventures** – Entrepreneurs can use policy loans to fund start-ups or expand existing businesses without dealing with traditional lenders and their high-interest rates.
- **College Tuition** – Parents and grandparents can use IUL loans to fund their children's education while allowing their money to continue growing, unlike 529 plans which have restrictions and tax implications.

By utilizing an IUL for these purposes, you gain greater control over your finances while keeping your money in a tax-advantaged and protected environment.

How to Eliminate Reliance on Banks and Lenders

The Infinite Banking Concept provides an opportunity to break free from the traditional banking system. Banks profit by lending out deposits at a higher interest rate than they pay their customers. Instead of contributing to this system, you can use an IUL to establish your own bank, keeping interest payments within your own financial ecosystem.

This approach helps you:

- Avoid high-interest bank loans
- Gain financial independence
- Create a reliable source of liquidity for future needs
- Pass down wealth through generations without tax burdens

Why Infinite Banking is a Tax-Free Wealth-Building Strategy

One of the most significant advantages of Infinite Banking is its tax benefits. When you borrow against your IUL policy, the IRS does not recognize it as taxable income. Additionally, the money inside the policy grows tax-deferred, and upon retirement, you can access it tax-free through policy loans. Furthermore, the death benefit is also tax-free, ensuring that wealth is transferred to future generations without unnecessary tax burdens.

By utilizing an IUL in this way, you gain access to a financial tool that provides liquidity, tax advantages, and long-term wealth-building potential. Infinite Banking isn't just for the ultra-wealthy—it's a strategy that anyone can implement to secure their financial future while eliminating reliance on banks and lenders.

Final Thoughts

The Infinite Banking Concept is a powerful tool that allows individuals to take control of their financial destiny. By leveraging an IUL policy, you can finance major purchases, build long-term wealth, and create a legacy that benefits future generations. Instead of working for banks, you become your own bank—gaining financial freedom, security, and peace of mind.

As you continue your journey toward financial independence, remember: *The money you control is the money that works for you.*

Chapter

9

UNDERSTANDING THE RULE OF 72 & THE PHASES OF RETIREMENT

The Rule of 72 – How Long Will It Take for Your Money to Double?

One of the simplest and most powerful tools for understanding how money grows over time is the **Rule of 72.** This rule states that if you divide 72 by your annual interest rate, the result is the approximate number of years it will take for your money to double.

For example, if you invest your money at an 8% annual return, your money will double in **9 years** (72 ÷ 8 = 9). If you put your money in a savings account with a 1% return, it would take **72 years** to double. Understanding this principle is crucial in making informed financial decisions, as it highlights the importance of seeking high-yield investments over time.

Why Traditional Savings Accounts Fail to Build Wealth

Many people rely on traditional savings accounts, thinking they are saving money efficiently. However, most banks offer interest rates below **1%**, meaning money in a savings account takes over **72 years** to double. Given the impact of inflation, which typically rises at **3% per year**, money in a traditional savings account is actually losing purchasing power over time.

Certificates of deposit (CDs) or money market accounts may offer slightly higher interest rates, around **2-3%**, but these still take **24-36 years** to double under the Rule of 72. For those aiming to retire within 20 to 30 years, relying solely on these options is not an effective wealth-building strategy.

How IUL Accelerates Compounding Compared to Banks and CDs

Indexed Universal Life (IUL) policies offer a unique advantage when it comes to compounding growth. Unlike savings accounts or CDs, IULs provide **market-linked**

returns without the risk of loss. Most IUL policies have the potential to earn **6-9% annually**, meaning money can double **every 8 to 12 years.**

Unlike traditional investments, an IUL policy also offers **tax-free growth** under IRS Code **7702**, further accelerating wealth accumulation. With an IUL, the cash value is not subject to annual taxes, allowing for compounding to take effect without the drag of taxation.

A Comparison of Stock Market vs. IUL Growth Using the Rule of 72

Many investors turn to the stock market for growth, as historically, the S&P 500 has averaged **8-10%** returns per year. Using the Rule of 72, this means investments in the stock market double **every 7-9 years.** However, stock market investments come with significant risk—market downturns can wipe out gains, and many investors struggle with timing the market effectively.

IULs, on the other hand, offer **market-linked growth** with a safety net. The **zero-loss floor** feature in IULs ensures that policyholders **never lose money due to market downturns.** While market gains can drive returns up to **10-12%**, the policy protects against crashes, making it a more stable option for those looking to build wealth without volatility.

The Phases of Retirement: Accumulation vs. Distribution

Retirement planning consists of two major phases: **Accumulation** and **Distribution**. Understanding these phases helps individuals plan their finances efficiently to ensure lifelong financial security.

The Accumulation Phase

The accumulation phase is the period when you are actively earning income and saving for retirement. This phase typically occurs between ages **20-60** and involves building assets through various investment vehicles such as:

- **Employer-sponsored retirement plans** (401(k), 403(b))
- **Individual Retirement Accounts (IRAs)**
- **Indexed Universal Life (IUL) Policies**
- **Stock market investments**
- **Real estate**

During this phase, the goal is to maximize **contributions, investment returns, and tax advantages**. Strategies include overfunding an IUL, making **consistent contributions**, and leveraging tax-deferred growth opportunities.

The Distribution Phase

The distribution phase begins when you retire and start drawing income from your accumulated assets. A common mistake is focusing solely on accumulation without planning how to **efficiently withdraw funds** without excessive taxation.

- **Traditional 401(k) and IRA accounts** are subject to required minimum distributions (RMDs) starting at age 73, meaning the IRS mandates withdrawals and taxes the income.
- **Social Security benefits** are taxed if combined income exceeds certain thresholds.
- **Tax-free IUL distributions** can supplement income **without increasing tax liability**.

IULs offer an advantage in the distribution phase because policy loans are **tax-free** under **IRC 72(e)** and **IRC 7702**, meaning retirees can access their cash value **without triggering taxable income.**

Why You Should Never Eat the Seed – The Importance of Protecting Principal

One of the key financial principles for retirement planning is to **never eat the seed.** The money you accumulate over time is like a **seed**—if you consume it all at once, it can never grow into something greater. Instead, you should focus on structured withdrawals that allow your wealth to continue growing.

Annuities, for example, function as a **money tree**, providing steady income in retirement while preserving the principal. Many retirees choose **fixed index annuities (FIAs)** to convert their accumulated wealth into **guaranteed lifetime income**, ensuring they never run out of money.

Why Insurance Companies Are More Secure Than Banks

A little-known fact is that insurance companies are often **20 times more secure than banks.** Unlike banks, which rely on the **Federal Deposit Insurance Corporation (FDIC)**—an entity that only insures up to **$250,000 per**

account—insurance companies operate under **strict financial reserve requirements.**

When banks fail, they rely on **insurance companies** to bail them out. Insurance companies hold large reserves and follow conservative investment strategies, making them far more stable in financial crises. This is why placing money in an IUL policy can be **safer than keeping it in a bank.**

Chapter 11

MONEY IS A SEED – NEVER EAT THE SEED

Annuities & Planting a Money Tree

One of the greatest financial principles is understanding that money is a seed. Just like a farmer would never eat all his seeds if he wants a future harvest, you should never consume all your financial resources without ensuring future growth. Annuities are one of the most powerful financial tools to help transform your savings into a lifetime income stream, allowing your wealth to grow and provide for you long after you stop working.

The Concept of Using Annuities to Create a Lifetime Income Stream

An annuity is a financial product designed to provide a steady income, typically during retirement. It acts as a personal pension, ensuring you never outlive your money. By placing funds into an annuity, you set yourself up for a consistent cash flow in the future, similar to receiving a paycheck for life. This is crucial because traditional savings accounts and employer-sponsored retirement plans, such as 401(k)s and 403(b)s, do not guarantee lifetime income. Annuities create financial security, protecting you from market downturns and longevity risk—the risk of outliving your savings.

How to Turn Your Savings into a Guaranteed Paycheck for Life

When you transition from the accumulation phase to the distribution phase of retirement, your financial goal shifts from growing wealth to ensuring a sustainable income. Annuities allow you to take a lump sum or periodic contributions and convert them into a guaranteed stream of income. This process, known as annuitization, ensures that no matter how long you live, you receive a consistent payment to cover your expenses.

The Difference Between Fixed, Indexed, and Variable Annuities

Understanding the different types of annuities will help you choose the best one for your financial goals:

1. **Fixed Annuities** – These provide a guaranteed interest rate and a steady, predictable income. They are ideal for those who want security and a low-risk investment.

2. **Indexed Annuities** – These are linked to a stock market index, such as the S&P 500. They offer the potential for higher returns than fixed annuities while providing downside protection, ensuring you don't lose money when the market declines.

3. **Variable Annuities** – These allow investments in mutual fund-like accounts, offering the potential for greater returns but also carrying the risk of market losses.

For those seeking stability and growth potential without market risk, **Fixed Index Annuities (FIAs)** are often the best option. They allow you to participate in market gains while ensuring you never lose your principal due to market downturns.

Using Annuity Ladders to Increase Income Over Time

Annuity ladders involve purchasing multiple annuities with different maturity dates or payout structures. This strategy helps you:

- Take advantage of changing interest rates.
- Ensure increasing income as you age.
- Maintain flexibility in financial planning.

By staggering annuity purchases over time, you create a system where income increases to keep pace with inflation and your changing needs.

Rolling Over 401(k) and 403(b) Accounts into Annuities

If you have money sitting in a 401(k) or 403(b) account, **do not start using that money immediately when you retire.** Instead, consider rolling these funds into a **Fixed Index Annuity (FIA)** a few years before retirement. This move allows you to protect your savings from market downturns while securing tax-deferred growth and guaranteed income.

Too many retirees make the mistake of withdrawing their 401(k) funds too soon, exposing themselves to high taxes, penalties, and market risks. By rolling your funds into an FIA, you ensure that your savings continue to work for you, providing a stable, predictable income throughout retirement.

Never Eat the Seed – Protect Your Wealth for the Future

Money in a savings account, sitting in the bank, or invested in volatile stocks should not be carelessly spent. **Never eat the seed.** Instead, plant it where it can grow and provide for you in the future. **Fixed Index Annuities offer a safe, tax-advantaged, and income-guaranteed way to preserve your wealth and create a financial legacy.**

If you want to retire with confidence, make sure you structure your savings in a way that allows for guaranteed income, tax advantages, and financial stability. By leveraging annuities and other smart financial tools, you create a money tree that will provide for you and your loved ones for generations to come.

Your Retirement Game Plan – Taking Action Now

The Power of Starting Early: Compound Interest & Tax-Free Growth

One of the greatest advantages in retirement planning is time. The earlier you start, the more powerful your money becomes, thanks to the magic of **compound interest** and **tax-free growth** within an **Indexed Universal Life (IUL) policy**. Compound interest is often referred to as the "eighth wonder of the world" because it allows your money to grow exponentially over time. When your savings generate earnings, and those earnings are reinvested to generate even more earnings, your wealth multiplies.

For example, let's compare two individuals:

- **Person A starts saving $500 per month in an IUL at age 25.** By the time they reach 65, assuming an average return of 7%, they will have accumulated over **$1.2 million** tax-free.

- **Person B waits until age 40 to start saving the same $500 per month.** By age 65, they will have accumulated only **$300,000.**

The difference is staggering, and it highlights a simple truth: **the earlier you start, the less you have to save to**

reach your financial goals. If you delay, you will have to contribute significantly more to achieve the same outcome. However, if you are starting late, don't be discouraged. The best time to start was yesterday; the second-best time is today.

Common Myths & Objections About IUL (Debunked)

Many people hesitate to take action on an IUL policy due to misconceptions or misinformation. Let's address some of the most common myths:

Myth #1: "IUL is too expensive."

Reality: IUL is customizable to fit different budgets. While maximizing contributions leads to faster growth, even modest amounts can accumulate significant tax-free wealth over time. The key is **starting where you are** and increasing contributions as your income grows.

Myth #2: "I'll get better returns in the stock market."

Reality: While the stock market has historically provided strong returns, it comes with **high volatility and risk.** An IUL policy is designed to protect your principal from losses while still allowing participation in market gains through index-based returns. During stock market crashes, your IUL account remains secure, avoiding devastating losses.

Myth #3: "IUL policies are too complicated."

Reality: Any financial tool can seem complex at first, but with proper education and guidance, an IUL is **one of the most powerful wealth-building strategies available.** A financial expert can help structure your policy for optimal growth and flexibility.

Myth #4: "I'll just rely on my 401(k) or IRA."

Reality: Traditional retirement accounts are **tax-deferred,** meaning you'll pay taxes on your withdrawals in retirement. With an IUL, your distributions are **tax-free,** allowing you to keep more of your wealth. Additionally, 401(k) and IRA accounts have contribution limits and penalties for early withdrawals, whereas an IUL provides more flexibility.

How to Combine IUL with Other Wealth-Building Strategies

A well-rounded retirement plan isn't about choosing **only one** financial tool; it's about combining strategies for **maximum efficiency.** Here's how an IUL can complement other wealth-building vehicles:

1. IUL + 401(k) or IRA

- Max out your employer's 401(k) match (if available) to take advantage of free money.

- Use IUL as an additional tax-free income stream, avoiding tax burdens on traditional retirement accounts.

2. IUL + Real Estate Investing

- Use policy loans from your IUL to **fund down payments** on rental properties.
- As rental income grows, repay the policy loan while still allowing your IUL's cash value to **compound uninterrupted**.

3. IUL + Business Ownership

- Business owners can **self-finance** through an IUL, avoiding bank loans and high interest rates.
- Use policy loans to fund expansions, buy equipment, or invest in marketing, all while keeping your money growing.

4. IUL + Infinite Banking Concept

- Use an IUL as your own personal bank, borrowing against the cash value to **finance major purchases, fund college tuition, or start a business.**
- Unlike traditional bank loans, policy loans do not require credit checks and are **not taxed as income.**

Final Steps to Secure Your Financial Future & Retire Stress-Free

Taking action today can mean the difference between financial stress and financial freedom in retirement. Here are the steps you should take **right now**:

Step 1: Determine Your Retirement Goal

- How much do you need monthly to retire comfortably?
- Use the **FIN (Final Income Number) method** to calculate your retirement target.
- Factor in inflation, healthcare costs, and lifestyle expectations.

Step 2: Establish an IUL Policy That Fits Your Budget

- Work with a financial professional to design an IUL policy tailored to your retirement vision.
- Choose the right funding strategy (monthly contributions, lump-sum deposits, or both).

Step 3: Optimize Your Budget to Increase Savings

- Identify unnecessary expenses and redirect them into your IUL.

- Use the **50/30/20 Rule** or the **Multiply Your Age by 10 Rule** to determine how much you should be saving.

Step 4: Commit to Long-Term Financial Discipline

- Avoid the temptation to withdraw from your retirement savings early.
- Regularly review and adjust your policy to ensure **maximum growth and efficiency.**
- Stay educated on wealth-building strategies and tax-saving opportunities.

Step 5: Create Multiple Streams of Tax-Free Income

- Use IUL alongside other retirement tools for diversified income streams.
- Consider rolling over traditional retirement accounts into **Fixed Indexed Annuities** for guaranteed lifetime income.
- Leverage policy loans to fund investments while still allowing your money to grow.

Conclusion

YOUR FUTURE BEGINS NOW

The path to a **stress-free, tax-free retirement** is not just for the wealthy—it's available to anyone willing to take control of their financial future. The sooner you start, the easier the journey will be. An **Indexed Universal Life (IUL) policy** is one of the most powerful tools for creating generational wealth, ensuring financial security, and avoiding unnecessary taxes.

Most people wait too long to start planning for retirement, believing they'll have more time or that they'll figure it out later. The reality is, **procrastination is the biggest financial mistake you can make.** Whether you are in your 20s, 30s, 40s, or even 50s, the best time to take action is now.

Don't leave your retirement to chance. **Make a decision today that your future self will thank you for.** Schedule a consultation, build your plan, and start securing your legacy. **Retirement should be a time of peace and abundance, not stress and uncertainty.** It all starts with **one simple step: taking action now.**

One day, I sat down with a client who was earning $5,000 a month. He was in his early 50s and had a clear vision—he wanted to retire comfortably by the age of 70. However, when we calculated his FIN (Final Income Number), it became evident that he needed to save at least $1,500 per month to reach his goal. Upon hearing this, he sighed and shook his head. "Wilken," he said, "I don't know how I'm going to do that. I can barely keep up with my current expenses as it is."

I could see the concern on his face. Like many people, he believed that saving for retirement required earning more money. But in most cases, the solution isn't necessarily making more—it's managing what you already have. I assured him that we were going to figure this out together. We pulled out his bank statements, credit card transactions, and a notepad to break down his monthly spending.

As we went through his expenses line by line, the truth became clear: a significant portion of his income was being spent on things that didn't serve his long-term financial goals. He was paying for multiple streaming services, daily coffee runs, frequent takeout meals, and unused gym memberships. His car insurance was higher than necessary because he hadn't shopped around for a better rate in years. He was also making minimum payments on a credit card with a high interest rate, which was quietly eating away at his income every month.

"Let's take a step back," I told him. "If we just make a few small changes, we can find the money you need without making you feel like you're sacrificing your quality of life."

Over the next hour, we worked through his budget with a new mindset. We canceled three unused subscriptions, saving him $50 per month. By preparing more meals at home instead of eating out five times a week, he freed up another $300. We renegotiated his car insurance, which reduced his monthly payment by $80. We also developed a plan to pay off his credit card faster, saving him hundreds in interest over time. Instead of buying coffee every morning, he committed to brewing it at home, a simple change that saved him an additional $120 per month.

By the time we finished, he was shocked. We had successfully found over $1,500 in his budget—without him needing to work more hours or take on a second job. "Wow," he said, shaking his head in disbelief. "I honestly thought I didn't have the money to save. But it was there all along—I just wasn't paying attention to where it was going."

This is the reality for many people. You may think you don't have the money to save for retirement, but you'd be surprised how much of your income is slipping away on unnecessary expenses. The key isn't just making more—it's making smarter financial decisions with what you already have. With discipline and the right plan in place, financial freedom is within reach.

Recap of the Book:

UNLOCKING FINANCIAL FREEDOM WITH IUL

Introduction: The Power of Financial Planning with IUL

Throughout this book, we have explored the critical aspects of retirement planning, wealth building, and financial security. At the heart of this strategy is **Indexed Universal Life Insurance (IUL)**—a powerful tool that not only provides a death benefit but also serves as a tax-advantaged vehicle for accumulating wealth.

Many people struggle with the uncertainty of retirement, the risks associated with traditional investment options, and the burden of taxes. We have uncovered why IUL stands out as a **smart, secure, and strategic** approach to financial freedom. This recap will revisit the key points discussed, emphasizing how IUL can be the cornerstone of a stress-free retirement and a robust wealth-building plan.

What Is IUL?

Indexed Universal Life (IUL) insurance is a permanent life insurance policy that offers a **cash value component** tied to a market index (such as the S&P 500). Unlike traditional whole life insurance, IUL provides flexible premiums and allows policyholders to **accumulate cash value tax-free**, which can be accessed during retirement.

The main components of an IUL include:

- **Death Benefit** – Provides financial security for beneficiaries.
- **Cash Value Growth** – Grows based on index performance while avoiding market losses.
- **Tax Advantages** – Enjoy tax-free growth, withdrawals, and loans when structured correctly.
- **Living Benefits** – Access funds in case of critical illness or financial hardship.

Unlike traditional retirement plans like **401(k)s and IRAs**, IUL allows you to bypass the risks of **market volatility, rising taxes, and contribution limits** while securing a financial future that is protected from unforeseen challenges.

Who Can Qualify for an IUL?

One of the greatest benefits of IUL is that **it is accessible to a wide range of individuals.** However, there are a few key qualifications:

- **Age & Health** – Approval is based on underwriting, which includes age and medical history.
- **Income Level** – While IUL is most effective for high-income earners, anyone with disposable income can leverage it for future wealth.
- **Financial Goals** – Those looking to grow wealth tax-free, protect assets, and create generational wealth are ideal candidates.
- **Commitment** – IUL works best when funded consistently, either through a **lump sum deposit or scheduled contributions.**

Even if you have pre-existing health conditions, there are **policy options available**, though premiums may vary. The key is to get started **as early as possible** to maximize the benefits of compound interest.

The Benefits of IUL

IUL offers several **unmatched benefits** that set it apart from other financial strategies:

1. **Tax-Free Growth & Withdrawals** – Unlike 401(k)s and traditional IRAs, which are taxed upon withdrawal, IUL allows you to access funds without tax penalties.
2. **Market Protection** – While it is linked to stock market performance, an IUL has a **floor rate** that ensures you never lose money in a market downturn.
3. **Flexibility & Liquidity** – Unlike fixed annuities or real estate, you can access funds from an IUL without stringent penalties.
4. **Protection Against Lawsuits & Garnishments** – In many states, the cash value in an IUL policy is shielded from creditors and legal judgments.
5. **Living Benefits** – If you are diagnosed with a terminal illness, chronic illness, or disability, IUL allows you to **access funds early**.
6. **Retirement Security** – Unlike traditional retirement plans, IUL allows you to enjoy **tax-free**

distributions, ensuring that your retirement income is maximized.

IUL and Retirement Planning

One of the most **misunderstood aspects of retirement** is the impact of taxes and inflation. Many people assume that their 401(k) or Social Security will be sufficient, only to find themselves struggling due to **rising tax rates, healthcare costs, and longer lifespans.**

How IUL Solves the Retirement Crisis:

- **Tax-Free Income** – While Social Security and 401(k) withdrawals are taxable, IUL loans are **not subject to income tax.**
- **Market Protection** – Unlike stock-based retirement accounts, IUL ensures that your wealth is not wiped out during economic downturns.
- **No Contribution Limits** – Unlike Roth IRAs, which cap contributions, IUL allows you to put in as much as you want.

- **Wealth Transfer** – Unlike 401(k)s, which are subject to estate taxes, an IUL provides a **tax-free inheritance** to your heirs.

IUL is **not just for retirement—it is a comprehensive financial solution** that allows individuals to grow their money, protect their assets, and pass on wealth without the burden of heavy taxation.

Other Key Concepts Covered in the Book

Beyond IUL, we explored **several critical financial concepts** that contribute to long-term wealth accumulation and retirement success:

1. **The Rule of 72** – A simple formula that determines how long it will take for your money to double based on a given interest rate.
2. **The Infinite Banking Concept** – How the wealthy use **life insurance as a personal bank**, financing major purchases and investments while keeping money growing.
3. **The Importance of Budgeting** – Strategies like the **50/30/20 rule** and saving **10x your age per month** to ensure financial security.

4. **Why Traditional Plans Fail** – The pitfalls of relying solely on Social Security, 401(k)s, and IRAs.

5. **Annuities & Money Trees** – How rolling over funds from a 401(k) or 403(b) into a **Fixed Index Annuity (FIA)** can provide lifetime income security.

6. **The Right Mindset About Money** – How poor, middle-class, and wealthy individuals think differently about money and how that impacts their financial future.

Final Takeaway: Take Action Now

The biggest financial mistake most people make is **waiting too long to start.** The power of **compounding interest, tax-free growth, and proper financial planning** lies in **starting early and staying consistent.**

- **If you're young, now is the time to begin funding an** IUL to take full advantage of compound interest.
- **If you're close to retirement, consider rolling over funds into an** IUL **or annuity** to maximize your tax-free income.

- **Regardless of your stage in life, financial literacy and taking action are key to securing your future.**

This book was written to **empower you with knowledge** and give you the tools needed to build a secure financial future. The next step is to **take action, consult a financial professional, and implement these strategies** to create the retirement you deserve.

By leveraging **Indexed Universal Life Insurance**, budgeting effectively, understanding tax laws, and applying wealth-building strategies, you can achieve financial independence and retire with confidence. **The future belongs to those who prepare for it today.**

Closing Thought

Retirement is not an age; it is a financial condition. Whether you are **25, 45, or 65**, the time to start planning is now. **You hold the keys to your financial destiny—make the decision to unlock a tax-free, secure, and abundant retirement.**

Biblical Wealth-Building Strategies – Timeless Principles for Financial Success

The Bible is filled with wisdom on building wealth, managing finances, and preparing for the future. Many of the wealth-building strategies used by successful people today are deeply rooted in biblical principles. Let's explore some key lessons from the Bible about wealth creation, stewardship, and financial security.

---

1. The Power of Diligence and Hard Work

Proverbs 10:4 – *"Lazy hands make for poverty, but diligent hands bring wealth."*

One of the most fundamental principles of biblical wealth-building is hard work. The Bible consistently teaches that wealth is not acquired through shortcuts or schemes but through diligence, persistence, and integrity.

Example: **Joseph's Story** (Genesis 39-41)

Joseph went from being a slave to becoming the second most powerful man in Egypt because of his diligence, wisdom, and ability to manage resources. He stored grain during years of abundance, which later allowed Egypt to survive a famine and profit from trading with other nations.

Lesson: Work hard, develop skills, and manage resources wisely to build sustainable wealth.

---

2. The Principle of Saving & Investing

Proverbs 21:20 – *"The wise store up choice food and olive oil, but fools gulp theirs down."*

The Bible warns against reckless spending and encourages saving for the future. Many people struggle financially because they spend everything they earn without setting aside anything for emergencies or investments.

Example: **The Parable of the Talents** (Matthew 25:14-30)

Jesus tells the story of a master who gave three servants different amounts of money (talents). Two servants invested and multiplied their money, while the third buried it out of fear. The master praised the ones who grew their wealth and condemned the one who did nothing.

Lesson: Money should not sit idle; it should be invested wisely to grow and multiply.

---

3. Diversifying Wealth – Gold, Silver, and Land

Ecclesiastes 11:2 – *"Invest in seven ventures, yes, in eight; you do not know what disaster may come upon the land."*

This verse advises spreading wealth across multiple assets to protect against financial risks. In biblical times, wealth was stored in **gold, silver, land, livestock, and trade goods.** Today, this translates to **stocks, real estate, business investments, precious metals, and life insurance policies** like an IUL.

Example: **Abraham's Wealth** (Genesis 13:2)

Abraham was very wealthy in **livestock, silver, and gold.** He understood the importance of **owning tangible assets** and not relying on a single source of income.

Lesson: Don't put all your money in one place. Build diverse streams of income and store wealth in assets that retain value.

---

4. Avoiding Debt & Living Below Your Means

Proverbs 22:7 – *"The rich rule over the poor, and the borrower is slave to the lender."*

The Bible warns against excessive debt, which can trap people in financial slavery. Many people struggle because they finance a lifestyle they can't afford, keeping them stuck in a paycheck-to-paycheck cycle.

Example: **Elisha and the Widow's Oil** (2 Kings 4:1-7)

A widow was drowning in debt, and creditors were coming to take her children as slaves. Elisha told her to **use what she had (a jar of oil), multiply it, and sell it to pay off her debts.**

Lesson: Avoid unnecessary debt and **focus on increasing your income and assets** instead of relying on loans and credit.

---

5. Tithing & Generosity – The Key to Financial Blessing

Malachi 3:10 – *"Bring the whole tithe into the storehouse, that there may be food in my house. Test me in this," says the Lord Almighty, "and see if I will not throw open the floodgates of heaven and pour out so much blessing that there will not be room enough to store it."*

Tithing is a principle where believers give **10% of their income** to God. This act of faith invites financial blessings and ensures that we **keep God first in our finances.**

Example: **Solomon's Wealth** (1 Kings 3:3-14)

Solomon gave generously to God, and in return, he was blessed with **wisdom, honor, and wealth beyond measure.**

Lesson: Giving is a spiritual law. When you give, you open the doors for more financial blessings.

---

6. Building Generational Wealth

Proverbs 13:22 – *"A good person leaves an inheritance for their children's children."*

True wealth is not just about making money for yourself—it's about creating financial security for future generations. Many people today **pass down debt**, while wealthy families pass down **assets, businesses, and financial wisdom**.

Example: **Jacob's Blessing to His Sons** (Genesis 49)

Before Jacob died, he gave each of his sons an inheritance and a blessing, ensuring that his family's wealth and legacy would continue.

Lesson: Don't just think about short-term financial goals—build a long-term financial plan that benefits your children and grandchildren.

---

7. The Power of Wisdom & Seeking Financial Knowledge

Proverbs 4:7 – *"The beginning of wisdom is this: Get wisdom. Though it cost all you have, get understanding."*

The Bible encourages learning and gaining financial knowledge. Many people struggle because they lack financial education. The wealthy **invest time and money into learning about wealth-building strategies**, while the poor often ignore financial literacy.

Example: **King Solomon's Wisdom**

Solomon didn't ask God for money—he asked for **wisdom.** As a result, he became the richest and wisest man of his time.

Lesson: Study financial principles, read books, and seek mentors who can help you grow your wealth.

Final Thoughts – Applying Biblical Wealth Strategies Today

Biblical principles for wealth-building are timeless. They emphasize **hard work, wise investing, avoiding debt, saving, generosity, and long-term planning.** Here's how you can apply them today:

1. **Work hard & develop a high-income skill** – Use your talents wisely.
2. **Save & invest** – Don't just save money; make it grow through investments like an IUL, real estate, and businesses.
3. **Diversify your assets** – Own cash-flowing businesses, land, and precious metals.
4. **Avoid unnecessary debt** – Don't become a slave to lenders.
5. **Tithe & be generous** – Give to open the doors of financial blessings.
6. **Build generational wealth** – Plan for your children's future.
7. **Continue learning** – Financial education is key to growing and protecting your wealth.

By following these **biblical wealth-building strategies**, you can create financial security, achieve financial independence, and leave a lasting legacy for generations to come.

QUESTIONS AND ANSWERS:

Why Each Person Should Have Their Own IUL Policy Instead of Adding a Spouse or Child Rider

When structuring an **Indexed Universal Life (IUL) policy**, many people wonder if they should add a **spouse rider** or **child rider** instead of purchasing separate policies for each family member. While a rider may seem like a cost-effective solution, it comes with **limitations** that could impact long-term financial security, wealth-building potential, and retirement planning.

1. IULs Are Designed for Wealth Accumulation – Riders Limit Growth

One of the **biggest advantages** of an IUL is its ability to **build cash value** over time through **indexed growth.** When each person has their own IUL policy, they maximize their ability to contribute additional funds into the cash value portion, which can be accessed tax-free later in life.

→ **Example:** If a couple has two separate IUL policies, they **each** have the ability to **overfund** their policy, taking full advantage of **compounding growth** and **tax-free withdrawals** in retirement. But if one spouse is simply added as a rider, they miss out on this opportunity to build wealth individually.

2. Riders Provide Limited Coverage and No Cash Value Growth

A **spouse rider** only provides a **small** amount of **death benefit coverage**, but **does not accumulate cash value.** IULs are **not just about life insurance**—they are also a powerful tool for **tax-free retirement income.** When you rely on a rider, you're **not building a financial future** for both spouses, only the primary insured.

→ **Stat: According to LIMRA, 40% of Americans worry about outliving their retirement savings.** Having **separate IULs** helps prevent this by ensuring each person has a **dedicated policy** growing cash value.

3. Independence & Policy Control

A **rider is dependent** on the primary policyholder. If the primary insured cancels the policy, **the spouse's coverage disappears.** With **separate IULs,** each person has their own policy, ensuring financial security no matter what happens.

→ **Example:** If a husband owns an IUL policy with a **spouse rider** and he **passes away,** the spouse **loses their**

coverage. If they had their own IUL, their policy would remain active and continue to grow tax-free.

4. More Control Over Retirement & Loans

IUL policies allow **tax-free loans** against the cash value for **retirement, real estate, business ventures, or emergencies.** If both spouses share one policy, they must **share** the cash value. Having **separate** IUL policies means each person can build their own wealth and use it as needed.

→ **Example:** A husband uses his IUL to fund an investment property, while his wife uses hers to supplement her retirement income. With **two separate IULs**, they **double** their financial options.

5. Child Riders vs. Individual IUL Policies for Kids

A **child rider** provides **small** coverage but does not build cash value. Instead, setting up an **IUL for a child** can give them **decades of tax-free compounding growth**, allowing them to access funds for **college, a home, or retirement.**

→ **Stat: A $100/month IUL contribution for a newborn could grow to over $1 million tax-free by retirement.**

Conclusion: Each Person Needs Their Own IUL Policy

While **spouse and child riders** may seem like a convenient way to get coverage, they **fail to provide the full benefits of an IUL**—namely **cash value growth, retirement security, and policy independence.**

For **maximum tax-free wealth accumulation, long-term financial security,** and **independent control over retirement income,** it's always better to have **separate IUL policies** instead of adding riders

2. What is the true rate of return after fees, caps, and participation rates?

The **actual return** of an IUL depends on several factors:

- **Cap Rate:** The maximum return you can earn in a given year (e.g., if the cap is **10%** and the S&P 500 grows by 15%, you only receive 10%).
- **Participation Rate:** The percentage of the index growth you receive (e.g., if the participation rate is **80%**, and the index grows by 10%, you get **8%**).
- **Spread Rate:** Some policies subtract a **spread** (e.g., **2%**) from your gains.
- **Fees:** Fees include cost of insurance (COI), policy admin fees, and rider charges. These **vary by policy and age**, but typically range between **1-3% annually.**

Example Calculation:

- S&P 500 grows by **12%** in a given year.
- Your IUL has a **cap of 10%** and a **participation rate of 80%.**
- You earn **9.6%** (80% of 12%), but the cap limits you to **10%.**
- After fees of **2%**, your net return is around **8%.**

Long-Term Rate of Return:

On average, **well-structured IULs generate 5-8% annual returns** net of fees over time. **While this is lower than an aggressive stock portfolio, the trade-off is guaranteed protection from market crashes.**

---

3. Can an IUL truly outperform traditional investment strategies, or does it just provide downside protection at the cost of lower gains?

This depends on **the investor's goals.**

Where an IUL Wins:

- **Market Crash Protection:** An IUL will never lose money due to market declines, whereas a mutual fund could lose **30-50%** in a bad year.

- **Tax-Free Growth & Withdrawals:** Mutual funds and 401(k)s are **taxed on withdrawals**, while **IUL loans are tax-free** if structured correctly.
- **No Required Minimum Distributions (RMDs):** Unlike a traditional IRA or 401(k), you can **control when and how much you take from an IUL.**
- **Legacy Planning:** IULs provide a **death benefit** that mutual funds do not.

Where an IUL Falls Short:

- **Lower Long-Term Growth Potential:** A mutual fund or ETF **without caps** can **outperform** an IUL over 30+ years in a **bull market.**
- **Requires Proper Structuring:** If not designed correctly, an IUL can be **expensive and inefficient.**

Who Should Consider an IUL Over Traditional Investments?

- **Those who want guaranteed protection against losses** while still participating in market growth.
- **People looking for tax-free retirement income.**
- **High-income earners** who have maxed out their 401(k) or IRA and need additional tax-advantaged savings.

- **Individuals who value liquidity** – IULs allow you to **borrow against your cash value tax-free** anytime.

Final Verdict

An IUL **is not meant to "beat" the market** but rather to provide **consistent, tax-free, market-linked growth with no downside risk.** If used **strategically alongside traditional investments,** an IUL can be a **powerful wealth-building tool.**

What happens if I miss a payment or underfund my IUL?

An **Indexed Universal Life (IUL) policy** offers flexibility, but missing payments or underfunding can have serious consequences depending on how the policy is structured.

Here's what happens if you miss payments or underfund your IUL:

Short-Term Flexibility: Unlike traditional whole life policies, an IUL **does not require fixed premiums.** If you miss a payment, the policy will use **cash value** to cover the cost of insurance (COI) and administrative fees.

Risk of Lapse: If there isn't enough cash value in the policy to cover fees and insurance costs, the policy may **lapse,** meaning you lose coverage and any potential benefits.

Catch-Up Contributions: If you underfund the policy, you can **increase future contributions** (if you haven't hit the IRS-imposed MEC limit) to make up for the shortfall.

Solution: A **properly designed** IUL should have a buffer of cash value to cover premiums if you miss a payment. This is why **overfunding** in the early years is recommended—it helps protect against unexpected income fluctuations.

---

2. Is it better to overfund an IUL aggressively, or should I spread my money into multiple investment vehicles?

This depends on your **financial goals, risk tolerance, and tax strategy.**

Advantages of Overfunding an IUL Aggressively:

- **Maximizes Tax-Free Growth:** The more you contribute (without exceeding MEC limits), the more cash value can grow **tax-free.**
- **Increases Borrowing Power:** A well-funded IUL allows you to **access tax-free loans** for retirement, business investments, or emergencies.
- **Provides Market Protection:** Unlike stocks or mutual funds, your money is **protected from**

market losses while still participating in market gains.

---

3. Can I add more money to my IUL over time, or am I limited based on my initial policy setup?

Yes, you can **increase contributions over time**, but there are limits and rules to follow.

How Additional Contributions Work:

Flexible Premiums: You can contribute more money to your IUL **at any time** as long as the policy is structured correctly and remains below the MEC (Modified Endowment Contract) limit.

Overfunding Within IRS Limits: The IRS limits how much you can contribute before the policy becomes a **MEC**, which would eliminate its tax-free loan benefits. A properly structured IUL maximizes contributions **without triggering MEC status.**

Adjusting the Death Benefit to Allow More Contributions: If you want to **increase contributions beyond initial limits**, you may need to **raise the death benefit** to accommodate higher premium payments.

Restrictions to Consider:

- Some policies may have **carrier-imposed limits** on how much you can contribute beyond your initial plan.
- If your IUL is already max-funded, you may need to open **a second policy** or use **other tax-advantaged accounts (e.g., Roth IRA, real estate, or private equity investments)** for additional savings.

If I borrow from my IUL, do I have to pay it back, and what happens if I don't?

One of the biggest advantages of an IUL policy is that you can **borrow against your cash value** without having to qualify for a traditional loan. However, whether or not you repay the loan will impact your policy in several ways.

What Happens When You Take a Loan from Your IUL?

- The insurance company lends you money using **your cash value as collateral.**
- Your policy's **cash value continues to earn interest** as if you never took the loan (depending on the type of loan you select).
- You are **not required to pay the loan back**, but unpaid loans will accrue interest over time.

What Happens If You Don't Pay It Back?

No Credit Impact: IUL policy loans do **not** appear on your credit report, so defaulting does not affect your credit score.

Loan Interest Accumulates: If left unpaid, loan interest continues to compound, **reducing your available cash value** over time.

Death Benefit Reduction: If you pass away with an outstanding loan, the amount owed (plus interest) is **deducted from the death benefit**, leaving your beneficiaries with less money.

Policy Lapse Risk: If the loan and accumulated interest grow so large that they **exceed the cash value**, the policy could lapse—potentially triggering a **taxable event.**

Expert Recommendation: While you're **not required** to pay back the loan, it's financially wise to do so **to protect the longevity of your policy** and maintain a strong financial safety net.

---

2. How do loan interest rates work in an IUL? Do I risk negative amortization (where my loan grows faster than my cash value)?

Yes, interest is charged on IUL policy loans, and **if left unpaid**, the loan balance can grow over time due to compounding interest. This is called **negative amortization**, and it can put your policy at risk if not managed properly.

Types of IUL Loan Interest Rates:

1. **Fixed Rate Loans:** The insurance company charges a fixed interest rate (e.g., 5-6%) on the loan, providing **predictability** in loan costs.

2. **Variable Rate Loans:** The interest rate fluctuates based on market conditions, which can be risky if rates rise significantly.

3. **Zero-Cost or Wash Loans:** Some policies offer a "wash" or "zero-cost" loan after a certain number of years, where the loan rate **equals the credited interest rate**, minimizing cost.

Can My Loan Balance Grow Faster Than My Cash Value?

Yes, this can happen if:

- The loan interest rate **exceeds the credited interest rate** on the policy.

- The policyholder **does not make payments** to cover accumulating loan interest.
- The **market underperforms**, resulting in lower cash value growth while the loan continues to compound.

Expert Strategy:

- Choose a **loan option** where your cash value continues to grow, offsetting loan costs.
- Avoid borrowing **too much too quickly**, which could outpace policy growth.
- Make **partial payments** toward loan interest to prevent compounding debt.

---

3. What happens if my policy loan balance exceeds my cash value? Could my policy lapse?

Yes, if the **loan balance and interest exceed the total cash value**, your policy is at risk of lapsing.

What Happens If an IUL Policy Lapses Due to an Unpaid Loan?

Loss of Coverage: Your life insurance policy will terminate, meaning your beneficiaries receive **no death benefit.**

Tax Consequences: If your policy lapses with a loan balance, the IRS may consider the loan as a **taxable distribution**, and you may owe taxes on the amount withdrawn.

Lost Investment Opportunity: Your accumulated cash value is gone, and you'll need to reapply for life insurance (likely at a **higher premium** due to age and health changes).

Expert Strategy:

- Keep an eye on your **loan-to-cash-value ratio**—don't let loans exceed **50-60% of your available cash value.**
- If you have a large loan, **consider repaying interest annually** to prevent compounding.
- Some policies offer **over-loan protection riders**, which help prevent policy lapse if your loan balance gets too high.

How do loan interest rates work in an IUL? Do I risk negative amortization (where my loan grows faster than my cash value)?

Yes, interest is charged on IUL policy loans, and **if left unpaid**, the loan balance can grow over time due to compounding interest. This is called **negative amortization**, and it can put your policy at risk if not managed properly.

Types of IUL Loan Interest Rates:

1. **Fixed Rate Loans:** The insurance company charges a fixed interest rate (e.g., 5-6%) on the loan, providing **predictability** in loan costs.
2. **Variable Rate Loans:** The interest rate fluctuates based on market conditions, which can be risky if rates rise significantly.
3. **Zero-Cost or Wash Loans:** Some policies offer a "wash" or "zero-cost" loan after a certain number of years, where the loan rate **equals the credited interest rate**, minimizing cost.

Who Decides What Indexes I Can Choose From, and Can They Change the Terms Later?

Insurance companies **control** the indexes offered within an IUL policy and can **adjust certain terms** over time.

Who Selects the Indexes?

- The insurance company provides **a list of indexes** (e.g., S&P 500, Nasdaq-100, MSCI Emerging Markets).
- Some companies offer **proprietary or volatility-controlled indexes,** which aim to manage risk.
- The policyholder selects which index (or combination of indexes) they want their cash value tied to.

Can the Insurance Company Change the Terms?

Yes, insurance companies typically **reserve the right to adjust:**

✓ **Caps:** May increase or decrease based on market conditions.
✓ **Participation Rates:** Can be adjusted up or down.
✓ **Spreads:** Some insurers increase spreads over time, reducing credited returns.
✓ **Index Options:** Insurance companies may add or remove indexes from their selection.

How to Protect Against Unfavorable Changes:

- Choose a company with **a strong history of maintaining high caps and participation rates.**

- Select policies with **multiple index options** for diversification.
- Regularly **review your policy** to ensure your index selections align with market conditions.

Expert Strategy:

- Work with a knowledgeable advisor who monitors insurance companies' **track records of adjusting caps and participation rates.**
- Diversify across **multiple index strategies** to reduce exposure to changes.
- Consider IUL policies with **fixed bonus crediting** options, which provide additional returns.

Final Takeaways

- **If the market crashes, your IUL won't lose money**, but it may not grow until the market recovers.
- **Caps, participation rates, and spreads directly impact your return**—choose policies with strong crediting features.

- **The insurance company controls index choices and can adjust terms**, so regular policy reviews are important.

Will My IUL Still Perform Well If I Live 30+ Years Into Retirement?

The long-term performance of an IUL depends on **proper structuring, disciplined funding, and strategic withdrawals**. If set up correctly, an IUL can provide a reliable source of **tax-free retirement income** for 30+ years.

Factors That Influence Long-Term Performance:

- ✓ **Consistent, Early Overfunding:** The earlier and more consistently you contribute, the more your cash value will grow, providing long-term sustainability.
- ✓ **Index Performance & Crediting Strategies:** While IULs are not directly invested in the stock market, their growth is tied to index performance. Diversifying among crediting strategies helps optimize returns over decades.
- ✓ **Proper Loan Management:** Policy loans allow you to access your cash tax-free, but mismanaging withdrawals can lead to unintended consequences.

Expert Strategy:

- Start **overfunding** the policy early to maximize compounding and buffer against low-crediting years.
- **Diversify index selections** to improve growth potential over time.
- Regularly review the policy to **adjust contributions and withdrawals** based on market conditions.

Why Should I Choose an IUL Over Real Estate, Stocks, or a Roth IRA?

Each of these financial tools serves a different purpose. **Real estate, stocks, and Roth IRAs** are excellent for building wealth, but an **IUL offers unique benefits that set it apart.**

- **Tax-Free Growth & Withdrawals:** Unlike traditional investments, an IUL **allows tax-free growth and access to cash through loans,** meaning you can use your money without triggering a taxable event.
- **Downside Protection:** Unlike stocks or real estate, **an IUL is not directly tied to the market.** When the market goes up, you earn interest based on

index performance. When the market crashes, your policy locks in previous gains and prevents losses.

- **Guaranteed Death Benefit**: Unlike stocks or real estate, an IUL **ensures a financial legacy** for heirs, no matter what happens to the market or economy.
- **No Contribution Limits:** A Roth IRA has strict IRS-imposed contribution limits, but an IUL **allows for higher contributions** (as long as it stays within IRS guidelines to avoid becoming a MEC).

While **real estate and stocks provide excellent growth potential**, they come with **market risk, taxation, and liquidity concerns.** A **properly structured IUL complements these investments** by providing a **safe, tax-efficient income stream** for retirement while protecting your wealth from market downturns.

Is an IUL a Good Option for Someone Who Is Already Maxing Out Their Retirement Accounts?

Yes, an **IUL is an excellent option for high-income earners** who have already maxed out their **401(k), Roth IRA, and other retirement plans**. Here's why:

- **No Contribution Limits:** Traditional retirement accounts have strict contribution limits, but an IUL allows for **higher contributions**, as long as it stays within IRS guidelines.

- **No Required Minimum Distributions (RMDs):** Unlike a 401(k), an **IUL does not require you to start withdrawing at age 73**, allowing your money to grow tax-free for as long as you need.
- **Tax-Free Access Before 59½:** Retirement accounts penalize early withdrawals. With an IUL, you can **borrow from your cash value at any age** without penalties.
- **Protection from Market Volatility**: Traditional investments in a 401(k) or Roth IRA **are market-dependent.** An IUL provides a **guaranteed floor,** meaning your money is safe even in a downturn.

For high-income earners who **need additional tax-free savings and wealth protection**, an **IUL is a powerful tool** to complement traditional retirement accounts.

Could I Achieve Similar Tax-Free Benefits Through a 529 Plan, HSA, or Municipal Bonds?

While **529 plans, HSAs, and municipal bonds** offer tax advantages, they are **limited in scope** compared to an IUL.

- **529 Plans:** These are excellent for saving for college, but **funds can only be used for education expenses**—otherwise, they incur penalties. An IUL provides **tax-free withdrawals for any purpose.**
- **Health Savings Accounts (HSAs):** HSAs offer tax-free growth for healthcare expenses, but **they have strict contribution limits and usage restrictions.** An IUL **allows for much greater contributions and flexibility.**
- **Municipal Bonds:** These provide tax-free interest, but **returns are generally lower**, and they do not offer **life insurance protection or wealth transfer benefits.**

An IUL offers **greater financial flexibility** and **tax-free wealth accumulation** while also providing **legacy protection** through a death benefit.

Takeaways

- **An IUL is a valuable complement to real estate, stocks, and Roth IRAs,** providing **tax-free growth, market protection, and a guaranteed death benefit.**

- High-income earners **who max out their retirement accounts** can use an IUL **for additional tax-free savings and liquidity.**
- While **529 plans, HSAs, and municipal bonds** offer tax advantages, **an IUL provides far greater flexibility** and wealth-building potential.

The best strategy? Use an IUL alongside other investment vehicles to create a **diversified, tax-efficient financial plan** that protects your wealth for the long term.

ABOUT THE AUTHOR

Wilken Dorcilien is a dedicated financial educator, entrepreneur, and motivational speaker with over a decade of experience in helping individuals and families build wealth, secure their financial future, and retire with peace of mind. As the founder and owner of *It's Possible Financial Services,* headquartered in Fayetteville, GA. he has empowered countless clients to take control of their financial destiny through strategic wealth-building solutions, including Indexed Universal Life (IUL) policies, tax-free retirement planning, and smart investment strategies.

Wilken is also the host of *The It's Possible Podcast,* where he shares valuable financial insights, personal development strategies, and interviews with industry experts to inspire listeners to achieve financial freedom. His passion for education stems from his own journey—growing up in Haiti, living in the Dominican Republic, and later moving to the United States, where he built his business from the ground up.

Beyond finance, Wilken is a sought-after motivational speaker, known for his engaging and practical approach to wealth-building and personal growth. His mission is simple: to help hardworking individuals break free from financial stress and create generational wealth. Through his books, seminars, and coaching, he continues to impact lives by showing that financial success isn't just possible—it's within reach.

Scan the code to book a call for IUL consultations:

SUBSCRIBE TO THE IT'S POSSIBLE PODCAST ON YOUTUTBE

BOOK ME NOW

MOTIVATIONAL SPEAKER

30 SECONDS
PLEASE WRAP
FINANCIAL
LITERACY
WORKSHOPS
Conventions
Church Programs
Community Events
Schools
Universities
BOOK WILKEN
770-470-2924
www.itspossibles.com
353 Glynn Street N,
Fayetteville, GA 30214
info@itspossibleinsurance.com

Made in the USA
Columbia, SC
26 March 2025

55704787R00115